TWAYNE'S WORLD AUTHORS SERIES

A Survey of the World's Literature

Sylvia E. Bowman, Indiana University

GENERAL EDITOR

GERMANY

Ulrich Weisstein, Indiana University

EDITOR

Sebastian Brant

(*TWAS 13*)

TWAYNE'S WORLD AUTHORS SERIES (TWAS)

*The purpose of TWAS is to survey the major writers
—novelists, dramatists, historians, poets, philosophers,
and critics—of the nations of the world. Among the
national literatures covered are those of Australia,
Canada, China, Eastern Europe, France, Germany,
Greece, India, Italy, Japan, Latin America, New Zea-
land, Poland, Russia, Scandinavia, Spain, and the
African nations, as well as Hebrew, Yiddish, and
Latin Classical literatures. This survey is comple-
mented by Twayne's United States Authors Series
and English Authors Series*

*The intent of each volume in these series is to present
a critical-analytical study of the works of the writer;
to include biographical and historical material that
may be necessary for understanding, appreciation,
and critical appraisal of the writer; and to present all
material in clear, concise English—but not to vitiate
the scholarly content of the work by doing so.*

Sebastian Brant

By EDWIN H. ZEYDEL

University of Cincinnati

Twayne Publishers, Inc. :: New York

Preface

Sebastian Brant ranks high among Western European writers of his time, and the role, however conservative, he played in an age marking one of the critical turning points in European history, was important. His masterpiece, the *Narrenschiff* (*Ship of Fools*), was the first book of a German author to enter the stream of European and world literature, leaving its imprint upon scores of writers in France and England. From the date of its first appearance in 1494 (two years after the first voyage of Columbus) to the present, new editions, reprints, translations into other languages, and adaptations have appeared on the average of one every six years. Under these circumstances it is surprising that his biography has never been essayed.

The sole attempt at a comprehensive study of Brant was made by the almost forgotten Alsatian scholar Charles Schmidt in his *Histoire littéraire de l'Alsace.* This comprises only a 140-page section in a general treatise on Alsatian literature of Brant's time, together with a thirty-page bibliography of his publications, the mere bulk of which indicates Brant's energy and suggests his impact upon the age. Moreover, Schmidt's work is written in French and is almost ninety years old. Schmidt's interpretation of the *Narrenschiff* and of Brant as a writer no longer has validity, and his assumption (to which a whole chapter is devoted) that Brant himself made woodcuts for the book, most of which actually were the work of Albrecht Dürer, was rejected many years ago.

Popular misconceptions about Brant and his *Narrenschiff* are still widespread, especially in the English-speaking world. Typical are two I have recently encountered that his masterpiece is a "medieval allegory," and that it is a pamphlet denouncing Church and clergy. Nothing could be further from the truth.

The present study, coming at the time of what may be an incipient Brant vogue both in Europe and in America, at least in scholarship, aims to fill a serious gap. Chapters 1 and 2 offer the principal facts concerning Brant's life and development as an early German Christian Humanist. The next four chapters discuss his writings as contributions to the intellectual life of his age. The last chapter represents an attempt to define his place in the world of the late fifteenth and early sixteenth centuries and to reveal his reactions to Humanism, as well as to such important events as the discovery of printing, the voyages of Columbus, the Turkish inroads in Europe, the rise and spread of Lutheranism, and the general spirit of unrest affecting even the Mother Church.

The Bibliography lists all those works to which reference is often made in the course of the discussion. Other less frequently used books are given in the Notes with full bibliographical information. However, the Bibliography does not list the works, editions, dedicatory introductions, poems, etc., by Brant himself. They comprise over eighty titles and would take up too much space. The Chronological Table lists the more important ones. A detailed and fairly complete catalogue of these is to be found in Schmidt's second volume, pp. 340–73, accessible in larger university libraries. Less complete is the list of Karl Goedeke in *Grundriss zur Geschichte der deutschen Dichtung*, secd. ed., I (1884), 381–92. Most of these items are referred to in the present volume.

Much of the information in Chapter Five concerning the impact of the *Narrenschiff* on the world at large is to be found in the introduction to my translation, *The Ship of Fools by Sebastian Brant*, now most conveniently accessible in the paperback edition of Dover Publications, Inc., of New York.

Besides using the considerable accumulation of published Brant research that has been appearing over a period of one hundred and forty years, I devoted much time during the summer of 1965 to research in the university libraries of Basel and Strasbourg—the cities in which Brant spent his life—as well as in the municipal archives of Strasbourg, where much Brant material is still to be found. The papers of the St. Thomas Foundation, now in the Strasbourg archives, were also used. Strasbourg is particularly rich in unpublished papers, Basel in early editions of Brant's works. I am grateful to the officials of these institutions for courtesies shown me and information offered, especially to Dr. F. Husner, librarian emeritus in Basel, also to M. J. Rott, librarian emeritus in Strasbourg, and M. Ph. Dollinger, director of the Strasbourg archives.

I am grateful to Professor Manfred Lemmer of the University of Halle, East Germany, and to Professor Ulrich Gaier of the University of California in Davis, for much valuable information. Some of the material in Chapter One on the cultural background of Basel in Brant's time is based on the research of Dr. William Gilbert presented in his unpublished Cornell dissertation. Helpful, too, was Dr. Charles E. Weber's University of Cincinnati typed dissertation *Catalog of the Incunabula in the German Language*, 1954.

I acknowledge my indebtedness also to Professor Bayard Quincy Morgan, the Stanford emeritus, for reading the manuscript and offering many valuable suggestions. Finally, I am grateful to Professor Ulrich Weisstein of Indiana University, and to Mr. Frank Kirk, the editor of the manuscript, for suggesting numerous improvements.

EDWIN H. ZEYDEL

Contents

SEBASTIAN BRANT

(1494-1521)

by

EDWIN H. ZEYDEL

Sebastian Brant is one of the most important European authors of his time. His life falls into the early period of German Humanism and ends four years after Luther posted his ninety-five theses in Wittenberg. Although he was a representative of Humanism, rather than Medievalism, he was a staunch adherent of the Mother Church. He wrote more than thirty works, some in Latin, some in German. His most important was the German *Ship of Fools,* which, provided with woodcuts by the famous Albrecht Dürer and others, was translated into six languages and influenced both French and English literatures significantly. Zeydel's study reappraises it and discusses it as a unique masterpiece—a well-constructed satire on contemporary society.

Zeydel's work is the first comprehensive study in any language of Brant's life and works, Latin as well as German, and is based primarily upon original painstaking research chiefly in Basel, Switzerland, and Strasbourg, France, where Brant spent his life and where most of the Brant material still available is found.

In 1944 Zeydel published the only extant English verse translation of the *Ship of Fools*—now to be had in a paperback edition published in 1962 by Dover in New York.

Chronology

Note: The principal works written or edited by Brant are included here. They, as well as others from his pen, are discussed in the chapters which follow.

1457 Probable year of Brant's birth.
Martin Mair's letter to Aeneas Sylvius.
1468 Death of Diebold Brant, the writer's father.
1475 Brant matriculates at the University of Basel.
1477 He is awarded the baccalaureate degree at Basel.
1484 Receives the license to teach and practice law in Basel.
1485 Marries Elisabeth Burg.
1487 Teaches Latin literature to a class in Basel, of which Locher is a member.
1489 Awarded the degree of *Doctor Utriusque Juris* in Basel.
He edits St. Augustine's *De civitate Dei* for Amerbach.
1490 Brant's law text *Expositiones sive declarationes . . .* appears in Basel, published by Furter. *Cato, Facetus, Moretus*, and *Thesmophagia* were probably translated into German by Brant (the first three published later).
1492 Columbus visits the New World for the first time.
1492– Dürer spends much time in Basel.
1494
1493 Maximilian is crowned Emperor.
Bergmann von Olpe opens his printing shop in Basel.
Brant edits the *Decretum Gratiani* for Froben.
1494 Bergmann publishes the first edition of Brant's *Narrenschiff*.
Brant edits *Bethicae et regni Granatae obsidio victoria et triumphus* in honor of King Ferdinand of Spain for Bergmann; appended to it is the Columbus letter on the explorer's first voyage (*De insulis in mari Indico nuper inventis*).

1495 Brant writes his *De origine et conversatione bonorum Regum.*

1496 Brant edits *Librorum Francisci Petrarchae . . . annotatio* for Amerbach.

1497 Brant edits Bebenburg's *Germanorum veterum principum zelus;* edits the works of Felix Hemmerlin, a forerunner of the *Narrenschiff;* and edits the works of Methodius and the complete Vulgate Bible for Petri and Froben.

The first edition of Locher's Latin adaptation of the *Narrenschiff* is published by Bergmann. The first Low German version of the *Narrenschiff* by van Ghetelen appears in Lübeck. The first French adaptation of the *Narrenschiff* by Rivière appears in Paris.

1498 The second French adaptation of the *Narrenschiff* by Drouyn appears in Lyons.

1499 The third French adaptation of the *Narrenschiff* appears anonymously in Paris.

Brant edits the Decrees of the Basel Church Council for that city.

1500 The first Dutch-Flemish edition of the *Narrenschiff,* published by G. Marchand, appears in Paris.

Brant edits Gazalupis' *De modo studendi in utroque jure* for Furter.

1501 Basel joins the Swiss Confederation.

Brant leaves Basel, settling in his native Strasbourg as legal adviser to the city council.

He edits the Fables of Aesop for Pforzheim in Basel.

After 1501   Brant composes his *Freiheitstafel.*

1502 Brant edits *Der heiligen leben,* an illustrated devotional, for Grüninger in Strasbourg. He edits *Hortulus animae,* a similar work, for Wehinger in Strasbourg. He also prepares an edition of Virgil, including numerous spurious works, for Grüninger.

He is summoned to Innsbruck by Emperor Maximilian as a consultant.

1503 Brant prepares an edition of Terence for Grüninger.

1504 He is promoted to be municipal secretary in Strasbourg.

1505 A second Latin adaptation of the *Narrenschiff,* by Badius, appears in Paris.

Chronology

1508   Brant edits Freidank's *Bescheidenheit* for Grüninger. He is called upon by Emperor Maximilian for expert advice in a matter concerning Venice.

1508–   Barclay's *Shyp of Folys*, the first English adaptation of the
1509   *Narrenschiff*, appears in London.

1509   Brant edits the *Layen Spiegel* for Otmar in Augsburg.

1513   He is again summoned by Emperor Maximilian for confidential advice. He completes his mission as mediator in the controversy on the immaculate conception (the case of Wigand Wirt).

1514   Brant and others greet and fete Erasmus in Strasbourg.

1516   Brant edits the *Clagspiegel* for Hupfuff in Strasbourg.

1517   As censor Brant must reject Murner's *Gäuchmatt*.
        Luther posts his ninety-five theses in Wittenberg.

1519   Emperor Maximilian dies.
        The revised second edition of the Low German *Narrenschiff* appears in Rostock.

1520   The Diet of Worms takes place.
        Brant heads a Strasbourg delegation to Ghent to pay homage to Emperor Charles V.

1521   April. He annotates a document concerning Luther—his last.

1521   May 10. Brant dies.

1532   Several works of Petrarch translated into German and published by Heinrich Steyner appear in Augsburg with a posthumous preface by Brant.

CHAPTER 1

Brant's Times and Early Life (1457-1494)

SEBASTIAN BRANT, occasionally referred to by his assumed
Latin name of Titio, or firebrand,[1] in accordance with the custom of his times, was probably born in 1457—if we accept as
literally correct the inscription on his tombstone, now set in a
wall of the St. Thomas Church of his native city of Strasbourg.
It states that he died on May 10, 1521, at the age of sixty-four.[2]
Other, less definite circumstantial evidence, as well as the much
later statement of Reussner in his *Icones* (1590) (offering one of
the extant likenesses of Brant, by Tobias Stimmer),[3] indicates 1458
as the year of his birth. The earlier date is to be preferred, unless
we interpret the tombstone inscription as meaning that he died in
in his sixty-fourth year; in this case 1458 could be correct. Modern
writers differ in their resolution of the question.[4]

I The Background

Brant lived in an age of transition, indeed one of the most critical ages in European history. It was the era in which Central
Europe began to feel the impact of Humanism, which had originated in Italy as early as the fourteenth century. To what extent
Brant came under the spell of Humanism, as it developed in the
countries north of the Alps, is one of the moot questions to which
these pages will be addressed. Humanism, in turn, sparked the
more pervasive Renaissance, or revival of learning, literature, and
art. And the Renaissance, for its part, was not without influence
upon the religious movement that strove to reform the Roman
Catholic Church and ended in establishing Protestantism. Brant's
relationship to the latter will also be discussed.

The times in which Brant lived are replete with significant
events that, in one way or another, reflect the mighty impulse of
some phase of these three great movements, each of which stems,

in the final analysis, from a single root. Only a few years before Brant's birth, the first books began coming off the presses of Europe—a noteworthy occurrence for his life and career. Even earlier than that, Greek fugitives had made the writers of ancient Greece better known in Italy and in the countries to the north. Greek influence became more noticeable after the fall of Constantinople in 1453, when more Greek scholars migrated to Western Europe.

Whether Brant was born in 1457 or 1458, his birth lies very close to the date (August 31, 1457) of the historic letter of the Mainz chancellor Martin Mair (or Mayr) to his friend Aeneas Sylvius. Mair, while congratulating Sylvius upon his elevation to the cardinalate, voices the strong complaint of the "German nation" against the absolutism of the Roman curia and its mulcting of the German people, coupled with the warning that the continuation of this policy would lead to a German defection from Rome. Mair writes: "Aroused suddenly from their sleep, as it were, our heads are now beginning gradually to think of means how they can remedy their misery; they are resolved to shake off the yoke and to return to their old freedom." [5]

This ominous warning was only one of the signs indicating the dawning of that epoch of profound reactions which marks the age into which Brant was born and signalizes the gradual breaking away of large parts of northern Europe from the Mother Church during his life. Brant was in his middle twenties when Martin Luther was born. When he was in his middle forties and had just left Basel for Strasbourg, the Swiss patriot and Protestant reformer Ulrich Zwingli arrived in Basel. Zwingli devoted himself to the study of theology under Thomas Wyttenbach; he was soon to start his career as a religious and political reformer. Zwingli was a defender of liberalism in theology, a foe of absolutism and of the sale of indulgences, an opponent of icons and most masses, and an advocate of marriage for priests. In 1517 Luther posted his ninety-five theses on the portals of the Wittenberg castle church and started the Protestant movement. His opponent Johann von Eck replied in 1518 with the *Obelisci* and in the next year engaged in disputations in Leipzig, first with Andreas Karlstadt and then with Martin Luther himself, who questioned the infallibility of the Council of Constance. Also in 1519, Zwingli began spreading from his pulpit in Zurich the doctrine of the Reformation, as he envisaged it. A year later Luther published his pamphlet *To the Christian Nobility of the German Nation,* which, thanks to its timeliness and the printing presses, had a tremendous dissemination throughout the vast German-speaking territories of that day. In 1521 Luther, summoned before the Diet of Worms, refused to recant and was declared a heretic. Finally, on May 4, 1521, six days before Brant's death, Luther was spirited away to the Wartburg.

It was also during Brant's life-span that the groundwork was laid for one of the most important achievements of the later Renaissance—the extension of the known physical world. When Brant was thirty-five, Columbus made his first crossing of the Atlantic and not only reached what turned out to be the New World, but also set the stage for the innumerable voyages of discovery and exploration that were to follow. And in 1507 the geographer and cosmographer Martin Waldseemüller, in his *Cosmographiae Introductio,* suggested the name for the newly found American continent.

Brant was intensely interested and involved in at least one of these phenomena, namely in the printing, publication, and writing of books and pamphlets. The explorations of Columbus, though completely misinterpreted by him, caught his passing attention, his disapproval stemming from a most peculiar reason.

Although he himself was much more proficient in Latin, he was also a student of Greek. Among his friends were Wimpheling, Reuchlin, and Erasmus, who were Grecists. In his chief work, *Das Narrenschiff,* Brant mentions scores of Greek heroes and heroines in Homer and other poets, among them Achilles and Patroclus, Orestes and Pylades, Agamemnon, Helen of Troy, and Penelope; philosophers like Socrates, Plato, and Aristotle; poets like Homer and Theocritus; and orators like Demosthenes. He also quotes Xenophon and Plutarch. But his knowledge of these figures stems, at least in part, from Latin sources.

The revival of learning, literature, and art also commanded his attention and interest, and he participated in it, insofar as it did not run counter to his religious, moral, and political scruples. An avid student and warm admirer of the Latin classics from a fifteenth-century point of view, he referred early in life to Terence, Catullus, Ovid, Virgil (his favorite ancient poet), and he knew the satires of Horace, Persius, and Juvenal. He cultivated a Latin style long before he had learned, by practice, to write lucid German. Manuscripts attracted him, as was natural at a time when printing was only a generation or two old. Later in life (1508) he published an illustrated edition and expansion of a thirteenth-century moralizing, sententious German poem by Freidank, *Bescheidenheit* (then meaning "experience" or "insight"), which furnishes evidence of his interest in literature in German. It is significant that he singled out this work, which has more down-to-earth popular appeal than almost any other German work of its time and may be mentioned in a breath with his own *Narrenschiff*.

However, the growth of Protestantism elicited but few striking comments from Brant, although he must have been aware of it and felt its import. His *Narrenschiff*, to be sure, came out about twenty-five years before the Reformation began. And during the last twenty years of his life in Strasbourg as legal adviser, city chancellor, secretary, and delegate on important political missions—as well as a leader of the local literary coterie—he was preoccupied with other matters and more or less pledged to silence on questions of state and church policy. But his close relationships with Johann Geiler von Kaisersberg and with a fellow Alsatian, Thomas Murner, indicate his involvement with public figures in religion. Geiler, whom Brant came to know well in Basel, became the most prominent clergyman in Strasbourg. Murner, eighteen years Brant's junior, was one of Brant's most fruitful imitators and, after 1521, was one of Luther's most bitter opponents. Strong Protestant currents were not felt in Strasbourg until Martin Butzer sought refuge there two years after Brant's death.

Actually, Brant was more concerned about the loosening of the bonds of the Holy Roman Empire because of internal disunity, as evidenced by Luther and Zwingli, and about the inability of the Empire to cope with the progress of the Turkish invaders than he was about the threat that Lutheranism and Zwinglianism posed. Indeed, when he died, he feared, but was not fully aware—as few contemporaries were—that the Protestant movement would lead to an irreconcilable break with the Church. The Turkish menace, but no basic ecclesiastical problem, was clearly in his mind when he wrote his *Narrenschiff* (especially Chapter 99) in 1494. It is generally true that his purpose was as much moral, satiric, and political as religious.

II *Brant's Youth*

Diebold Brant, the Younger, owner and keeper of the inn at the sign of the Golden Lion in Strasbourg, was Brant's father; his mother was Barbara Picker, often called "die Pickerin." His paternal grandfather, Diebold the Older, belonged to the Strasbourg wine-dealers' guild and enjoyed the esteem of his fellow citizens in the city of some twenty thousand inhabitants. He was elected member of the Great City Council eight times, the last time in 1461. Brant's father, the younger Diebold, died on Epiphany (January 6), 1468. At his death Sebastian, the oldest son, was barely ten years old, and there were at least two younger boys, Matthias (who became a printer), and Johann (who later took over his father's business). Barbara, a resolute woman, was successful in maintaining her home and educating her sons.

In a letter written to Reuchlin in 1484, Brant reveals his half-humorous attitude toward what seems to have been a poverty to which he was accustomed and which still haunted him. He writes: "I am restraining Fortune in her flight, I shall pursue her perchance, unless she, the dispenser of blessings, proves unwilling. . . . But I fear that one year or the next will resist my desires." [6] In 1498, again a few years later, the publisher Bergmann von Olpe testifies that Brant's economic condition was still precarious.[7] Not until he returned to his native Strasbourg did his finances cease to be a problem. This contradicts what Schmidt says (I, 192), but he adduces no proof that after 1468 the Brant family was free of financial worries.

In the absence of a good public school in Strasbourg at that time, Barbara made sacrifices to give her eldest, in whom she detected special intellectual gifts, the best education she could. At first he probably attended the parish school of the St. Thomas Church, then one in Baden. In addition, he had private teachers, one of these possibly the pedagogue Johann Müller, who had settled in the Alsatian capital, then still predominantly German. The statement, in a letter to Brant written by an anonymous adversary, that he had attended inferior private schools[8] is merely a studied slur on his education; indeed it is refuted by the tenor of Brant's reply.

There is no evidence that Brant ever attended the recently founded Humanistic Latin school of the Westphalian educator Ludwig Dringenberg in Schlettstadt in Lower Alsace, to which several early German Humanists, among them Peter Schott and Jacob Wimpheling, later also Erasmus, were attracted. Here *devotio moderna,* the new religious movement of complete submission to faith, from the Netherlands, was introduced. This school was a forerunner of such famous Latin schools as Schulpforta, St. Afra, and Grimma in Saxony, and Ilfeld in the Harz region, where centuries later leaders like Klopstock, Gellert, and Lessing laid the foundation of their education, and which in a sense played a more important part in the training and development of great intellectual leaders than did the universities. To be sure, in a letter of 1478 to Brant, Schott, the son of the Strasbourg *ammeister* ("mayor"), refers to their friendship as dating "from an early age." [9] But it is not likely that it points to school days spent there together.

Barbara not only afforded her son a good education, she also influenced him profoundly. Though an affectionate mother, she was a purposeful woman and impressed her character upon him. As we know Brant from his work, he reveals the innate sensitivity that probably also characterized her. And if sometimes he appears tenderly womanish, even testily so in some of his strictures, we may identify these traits as part of the heritage of his mother, who was in personal charge of his upbringing during his most impressionable years.

In the letter to Brant written in 1480 by the anonymous adversary, probably a Constance teacher named Wenceslas Brack (and pertinent also to his relationship to Humanism), insult after insult is hurled at him. He replies sharply in kind, yet at the end seeks the writer's friendship: "I swear I have never done you any harm publicly or privately, nor will I, unless attacked. Acknowledge your folly. . . . Don't always be a liar, a detractor, an accuser. Give all this up. . . . You will gladly seek acquaintance and friendship between us once you have found out how I really am." [10] This clearly indicates a sensitive but basically loving nature, a readiness to forgive and forget, and a craving for friendship. A few years before that he writes to Schott, seeking renewed assurances of his friendship, which elicits Schott's letter of 1478, just referred to. Schott replies: "As for your admonition that I preserve our friendship which as a youth, at an early age, I cultivated for you, who were also a youth—I grieve that you are so disposed as to think I must be exhorted in this manner; yet it was as unpleasant to me that my love for you was suspect as it was pleasant that you made the inquiry." [11] This involved passage bespeaks an attachment such as young girls might feel for each other, not to mention signs of shy distrustfulness.

A sense of shame that Brant felt all his life for having read the lewd pseudo-Virgilian poem *Priapus,* thinking that it was a genuine work of his favorite, is another example of his effeminate, moralistic attitude. The portraits we have of him reveal only too clearly the features of a stern moralist. If we needed further proof of his testiness and intolerance of even petty foibles, his *Narrenschiff* would supply it on almost every page.

But if Brant was also at times difficult, hypercritical, and vain, these were not necessarily traits inherited from his mother. We find that they were not uncommon among scholars in that period, so proud of its achievements. Whenever possible, Brant took credit publicly for whatever he wrote.

His contemporaries were aware of these weaknesses. Reference has been made to the anonymous letter of 1480. It will be discussed again in regard to his relation to Humanism, but it is pertinent here because it accuses him of being dogmatic and conceited. "Almost all other poets," the correspondent writes, "had models. Virgil had Homer, and Terence Menander. But you are a leader and an authority unto yourself. You don't consider any word rare unless it is not found anywhere. . . . That ostentatiousness, and the way you elevate yourself above others, is your own invention. Hence I have never accepted you as having had teachers that could make you so learned in the arts or the humanities as you boast you are." [12] This letter was signed only "N N N." Brant testily added "-ar" to each "N" (*Narr* = "fool").

Brant's lengthy reply to this charge shows his irritation, which is perhaps not unjustified. "By charging me with conceit," he exclaims, "and saying that I boast of being a poet or orator, you speak as do the most empty-headed people, who never hesitate to accuse others of their own faults." [13] He calls his correspondent a "fanatic beast." An early poem of Brant, "Ad invidum" ("To an envier"), preserved in the St. Thomas archives in Strasbourg, deals with the same adversary in an exaggerated rhetorical style, accusing him of execrable (*nefas*) conduct in compelling Brant to take weapons into his unwonted hands.[14] Suffice it to say that the views on education he expresses in his letter are more forward-looking than those of his opponent. His general feelings on this matter are found in Chapter 27 of his *Narrenschiff*. The students, he complains, carouse instead of studying, and the teachers prate empty sophistries:

> In Leipzig students act this way,
> In Erfurt, Mainz, Vienna ay,
> Heidelberg, Basel, any place . . .

He scolds the professors in these words:

> And teachers too endure this trouble,
> Sensible learning they'll not heed,
> Their talk is empty, vain indeed.
> Could this be night, or is it day?
> Did mankind fashion monkeys, pray?
> Was't Plato, Socrates who ran?
> Such is our modern teaching plan.
> Are they not bred to folly true
> Who night and day with great ado
> Thus plague themselves and other men? [15]

The traits of character we find in Brant were not all bad by any means. He was steadfast in his principles, trustworthy, and loyal to his friends and to Church and Empire, zealous in everything he undertook, conscientious, sincere in his convictions, and dedicated to his ideals.

Peter Schott, the young Humanist, who has been mentioned as one of Brant's earliest friends, attended the new Humanist school established by Dringenberg in Schlettstadt. Later he studied in Paris and Bologna and became an enthusiastic advocate of Humanism. His letter to Brant of 1478 reveals this enthusiasm. Brant probably shared it, and when in 1475 his mother sent him to the comparatively new University of Basel, he would have liked nothing better than to devote himself chiefly to the study of the Classics. He already had a good grounding in Latin before going to Basel.

In Basel, Brant enrolled in the "Humanistic" faculty, or "Artistenfakultät" (a prerequisite for the others), following a broad course of studies and devoting his time to philosophy, logic, physics, and rhetoric during his first two years. The Classics, not yet a recognized field of study, were read in connection with philosophy and rhetoric and contemporaneous as well as Church writers. "Poetics," however, was slowly becoming established. Greek was taught privately in Basel by one Andronicus Kontoblakas, and Brant was tutored in it by him, and in Latin as well as Greek by Johannes Reuchlin. The latter, about two years older than Brant, had moved from Paris to Basel in 1474.

Reuchlin and Brant became lifelong friends, although Brant did not always fully reciprocate Reuchlin's friendly devotion and, since Reuchlin was a Nominalist, disagreed with him on philosophical issues. However, he wrote several laudatory pieces on him in the 1490's, among them a dedication for Reuchlin's play *Scenica progymnasmata,* or *Henno* (1498), in which he calls him "sweet-tongued" and praises him for restoring comedy in Germany. In his letter of October 1, 1495, Brant assures Reuchlin that he alone can bring literary fame to Germany.[16]

About his knowledge of Greek, Brant says in the aforementioned letter of 1480 to his anonymous critic: ". . . the statement that you make about my mixing Greek with Latin—that I reject because, alas, I have only an elementary knowledge of Greek." [17] But he learned enough to use it effectively now and then[18] and doubtless read in the Greek authors.

Brant became the famulus, or attendant, of Professor Jacob Hugonis of Morsmünster (or Mauersmünster), who had Humanist interests and was also Reuchlin's teacher. Brant's poverty, already discussed, is also indicated by his service to Hugonis and by a university record in Basel stating: "he [Brant] paid nothing because he is a servant" (*nil solvit quia servitor*). But this was amended subsequently by "he paid later" (*postea solvit*) and by a note in 1477 that one florin was received "from a certain student living with Jacob Hugonis, now promoted to the baccalaureate" (with the name "Sebastiano Brant" in the margin).

The thoroughness of Brant's general preparation at home paid off, and in 1477 he secured the baccalaureate degree. In the same year Reuchlin was awarded his Master's diploma. He delivered the commencement address to the baccalaureates in Brant's class, speaking on philosophy as a guide to virtue.

Meanwhile Brant found time to browse among the manuscripts of the Carthusian monastery and commune with friends (e.g., Ludwig Moser and Johannes Heynlin). In the tradition of Humanism he also indulged his extracurricular literary tastes by writing a considerable amount of occasional Latin verse, becoming in due time a sort of unofficial poet laureate of Basel. His first volume of verse—almost entirely in honor of the Virgin Mary—appeared in 1494.[19] During these early Basel years he lived in the Bursa Hieronymi, regent Jerome Berlin's house, where Aristotelian logic was especially cultivated. The "Burses" were combination dormitories, refectories, and study and lecture halls.

III   *Activities in Basel*

Already at this time, Basel was a famous seat of the southwestern German Renaissance. The Basel Church Council of 1431–48, which reaffirmed the edicts of the Councils of Pisa (1409) and Constance (1414–18), established on paper the authority of the Church Assembly, or Synod, over that of the Pope. But in practice it failed to break the papal power.

The importance of this long, drawn-out Council for the cultural life of Basel can hardly be overestimated.[20] When Aeneas Sylvius, who was later to become Pope Pius II, wrote his letters from there in 1434 and 1438, he indicated that the cultural level of the town had not been high, although economic prosperity was noticeable, and the town seemed wide-awake and modern. But the Council effected a marked change. At times during the sessions, more than fifty cardinals, patriarchs, archbishops, and bishops were present. The universities were represented. Emperor Sigismund remained in Basel for more than six months and summoned the Reichstag there. In 1440 the antipope Felix V was crowned in Basel, and in 1442 the Roman King (a title of presumptive emperors) Frederick III came. The brilliant scholar Giuliano Cesarini served as the first

Council president and welcomed also the delegates of the Eastern Church. Humanists like Aeneas Sylvius, Louis d'Allemand, cardinal of Arles, Nicolaus Cusanus, and the apostolic prothonotary Gregoris Correr played prominent roles in the deliberations.

Several delegates took the occasion to make excursions to northern Germany in search of Greek and Latin manuscripts, using Niccolo Niccoli's *Commentarium* as a guide. As Aeneas Sylvius notes in a letter to Giovanni Peregallo, these men shed glory upon the little city, comparable to that of Athens. Indeed, one of the Greek delegates, Demetrios Paleologus Methotides took the time to teach some of his Western fellow delegates Greek. An attempt was even made to found a university in Basel during the later years of the Council. It existed from 1440 to 1449.

The Council, though ending inconclusively, contributed immensely to deepening the pride felt by the people of Basel for their city. It left them with indelible memories of glorious days and added political prestige to the town. What had been a small provincial city became during these years a cosmopolitan center ready to accept new ideas and novel ways. Brant published the Council's decrees in 1499.

There were other signs of a cultural awakening in Basel during the latter half of the fifteenth century. One was the active role the Carthusian monastery and its excellent library played in the community.[21] This library was actually the center of learning in Basel throughout most of that century, and perhaps the best administered in all of Germany. Founded in 1401, the monastery attracted scholars from all parts of Europe, especially from the north. Its library was enriched greatly during the Council by gifts of manuscripts, especially Greek, donated by grateful delegates housed in the monasteries. The early Basel presses, particularly that of Johann Amerbach, also helped by donating many of their precious tomes. The Carthusians also counted among their treasures numerous Classical-Humanistic works from the presses in Mainz, Rome, and Venice. They owed many of these to the good offices of one of their most prominent scholars, Johannes Heynlin, also called Von Stein. He gave the Carthusian monastery two hundred and thirty-three bound and some fifty unbound volumes, annotated by him, most of them now in the library of the University of Basel. He will be discussed below as a potent influence on Brant.

The Dominican monastery, also prominent in Basel, was some-what less influential

Another factor in the cultural life of fifteenth-century Basel was the university.[22] We have seen that the first university failed after only nine years, two reasons being the financial burden its opera-tion entailed and the letdown immediately after the conclusion of the Council. In 1460 a new, successful attempt was made to found a university. It was patterned on the University of Erfurt, which also supplied some of the professors. The chancellor was the bishop of Basel, the rector also a clergyman. The teaching of civil law, never before undertaken in a German university, was made possible by the importation (for a while) of professors from Italy.

At that time, an old scholastic quarrel between Dominicans and Franciscans was in its final stages. As a problem of Scholasticism it was a barren dispute concerning the relation of the abstract to the concrete, the Franciscans adhering to what is called Nominal-ism, the Dominicans to Realism. Nominalism held that all Uni-versals (abstract terms) are nothing but exigencies of thought or devices of language, and exist only as names with no realities be-hind them. The motto of Nominalism therefore was: "Universalia post rem" ("abstractions come after the thing itself"). Realism, on the other hand, contended that the Universals do have concrete reality, and its motto was: "Universalia ante rem" ("abstractions precede [or are inherent in] the thing itself). The former imag-ined Aristotle to be their ultimate authority; the latter, Plato.

By the middle of the fifteenth century the Nominalists had come to be identified with the party that opposed what it termed the encroachments of the Roman hierarchy, yet favored the old Scho-lastic education. The Realists, on the other hand, stood behind the policies of the Church and advocated a more liberal Humanistic approach to education.

In Basel, Nominalism served at first as the sole basis of instruc-tion in the philosophical faculty. But in 1464 three masters came from Paris, one of them Heynlin, who has already been mentioned, and introduced Realism. From the 1470's to 1492 the Humanistic, or philosophical, faculty was divided into two camps, each with its own dean and council. The Nominalist camp was the stronger. Among its members were Reuchlin, Lauber, and Hugonis, whom Brant served as a student. Most of Brant's friends, however, were

Realists, among them Surgant, Oiglin, and the future publisher Amerbach. The influence of this quarrel on Humanism is discussed in Chapter 7.

For a while during the 1470's the students could vote in university elections and even serve as rectors. They could also teach in one faculty while studying in another. Though not numerous, they came from all parts of Germany, as well as from Switzerland, France, and Bohemia. In the Humanistic faculty there was probably more stress on Humanism than at any other German university. Indeed, provision had been made for the humanities when the institution was founded. There was less ecclesiastical domination than elsewhere, and a good rapport between town and gown existed.

Among the early rectors with years of their incumbencies, with whom Brant came in contact were Wilhelm Dremborn (1475), Jacob Lauber (1476, 1477), Hugonis (1477), Bernhard Oiglin (1478, 1481, 1488, and 1496), Johann von Gengenbach (1481), and Johann Ulrich Surgant (1482 and 1487). In the "Rektoratsmatrikel" (I, 98), Brant glorified Oiglin in seven distichs when he assumed his fourth term.

Finally the activity of the printers and publishers was important.[23] Basel was one of the first cities to take up printing. It seems that some of its printers had come there from Mainz to escape political disturbances. The town offered them undoubted advantages. It had a university and was an episcopal city and religious center with a cathedral chapter; it was also a free imperial city and possessed several monasteries. Moreover, it could boast a lively commerce and a paper-making industry.

There has been much controversy about when printing activity actually began in Basel; it was probably around 1470. Among the better-known men who printed and published books there during the next generation or two were Johann Wenssler, Amerbach, Thomas Wolff, Johann Petri, Johann Froben, Michael Furter, Michael Kesler, and Bergmann von Olpe. They all enjoyed special privileges, being considered not artisans but artists. Some were occupied almost exclusively with woodcuts. Bergmann, a native of Westphalia, was independently wealthy and a fellow student of Brant's. Amerbach, a native of Reutlingen, had a Master's degree from the University of Paris; others had studied and worked in

Italy. Their books catered to a wide European market, and they kept in close touch with colleagues elsewhere. Amerbach and Bergmann probably had the greatest cultural impact. The former, who had studied under Heynlin in Paris and was strongly under his influence, had first worked as a printer in Nuremberg. He published, among other writings, those of the Church Fathers. Bergmann, who was trained at Furter's shop and for whom Brant often worked (but by no means exclusively), published books by Wimpheling, Reuchlin, several of Brant's works, including the *Narrenschiff*, as well as works by Locher. His motto was "Nüt ohn Ursach" ("Nothing without Cause"). A theologian by training, he became an archdeacon of the Church.

Several editions of the Vulgate Bible—one by Petri and Froben in 1498, and another by Froben, Petri, and Amerbach in 1498–1502—appeared in collaboration, a not uncommon practice. But no vernacular Bibles were published, and but few Latin or Greek classics, the latter being monopolized more or less by Italy. The comparatively few Humanistic books that did appear in Basel were probably intended for instructional purposes. Basel printers also issued theological writings, among them those of St. Augustine, sermons, works of edification, treatises on Mary and the saints, moral homilies, university textbooks, grammars, books on philosophy and canon law, the letter of Columbus to Sanchez (three times: twice by Bergmann and once by Wolff); also many works illustrated with woodcuts, often for the illiterate, including the *Narrenschiff* and the German *Ritter vom Turn* ("Knight of the Tower"), published by Furter from a French tale by the Chevalier de la Tour de Landry, and illustrated by Dürer.[24] In a lighter vein are Poggio's *Facetiae* and Brant's German translation of it.

The books published in Basel were rated highly, and with good reason. Toward the end of the century as many as one hundred and fifty persons were engaged in the book trade there. The principal buyers were churches, monasteries, parish priests (for their own use or, in the case of books in the vernacular, to read to their parishioners), schoolmasters, professors, students, and the literate laity in general. If Basel never published as many books as did Venice or Paris, it must be remembered that it was a smaller community.

One distinctive feature of Amerbach and Bergmann is their use of roman type even for German books—a mark of their conscious endeavor to cater to Humanistic circles outside of Germany.

Until 1501 Basel remained a part of the Holy Roman Empire and shared with Strasbourg the prestige of being the center of the southwest German Renaissance movement. Indeed, so far as alert intellectual life, vigorous development and productivity are concerned, the Christian-Humanistic culture of Basel of those days was probably superior to any other on German soil, be it in Cologne, along the Rhine, or in Swabia. Artists also felt at home there. Dürer visited Basel between 1492 and 1494, and Holbein the Younger somewhat later. This, then, was the environment in which Brant was privileged to live for some twenty-five years.

Brant did not drop his university studies in 1477 after receiving the baccalaureate degree—no longer granted in Germany today. For a while he thought of transferring to Freiburg but decided against it.

Probably Brant's own economic plight as well as that of his family at home necessitated academic pursuits that promised more remuneration. So he halfheartedly chose law,[25] the reluctance perhaps being caused by reasons similar to Reuchlin's, who felt that the law was too dependent upon men's whims, as well as upon bribery and artful words. His mother would have preferred him to elect theology.[26] Though he did not abandon the Classics, he now concentrated his studies upon canon and civil law. In dealing with canon law, for which Peter von Andlau was his principal professor,[27] he was of course engaged in a field very close to theology. We shall see that Andlau's philosophy influenced young Brant considerably, especially with regard to the relationship of Pope and Emperor.

During this time Brant was occasionally drawn into controversies that engulfed the Basel Humanists. Grave trouble, stirred up when in 1482 archbishop Andreas preached in the cathedral against the government of the Church, aroused him deeply, as Schmidt relates (I, 198f.). In the same year, as "king of the bean" at Twelfth Night, Brant composed a jolly piece (reprinted in the *Varia Carmina* and quoted below in Chapter 3), in which he called his own kingdom a realm of the pen and of hope, stressing his own impecuniousness.

Although Brant secured his license to practice and teach canon law, and incidentally also civil law, in 1484, he also taught "poetry" in the Humanistic faculty for many years. For a while he also practiced jurisprudence in Baden. By 1485, though still struggling to earn a living, he married Elisabeth Burg, or Burgis (also Bürgi), the daughter of a Basel cutler, by whom he had seven children. Schmidt (I, 209f.) adduces insufficient evidence to prove that the marriage was not happy.[28]

His eldest son, Onuphrius, was a most precocious lad, whom he brought up on Latin.[29] At the incredibly early age of seven he was matriculated as a student at the University of Basel. Later he studied at Freiburg and wrote occasional German verse of mediocre quality. By 1506 he held a subordinate post in the Strasbourg chancellery and then another similar position. Three times he was a member of the Great City Council. Sometimes he accompanied his father on journeys. Three daughters are also mentioned: Euphrosina, who married Matthis Pfarrer, a merchant and magistrate; Anna, who after losing her first husband, Jacob Gerbott, married Peter Butz, Brant's successor as chancellor in the Strasbourg government; and Magdalena, who remained single. Euphrosina's daughter Barbara married a Nicholaus Hugo Kniebs; and another of her daughters, Maria, a Stiblinus. Maria, in turn, had a daughter Elisabeth, who married a Jacob Schalter. The last male descendant of Brant, Johann Daniel, died in 1759.

In 1489 Brant secured the coveted degree of *Doctor utriusque Juris,* that is, of civil and canon law, an official notice of which is preserved among the Zarncke papers at Cornell University. Once he had this degree, the highest attainable, he was well established at the University and in town. In the same year he delivered the traditional address to the baccalaureate class, quoting frequently from Virgil and stressing man's superiority over beasts. He served as dean of the faculty of law in 1492.

With none of the intellectual leaders of Basel did Brant have closer relations than with Heynlin.[30] It has been noted that in 1464 Heynlin was one of three masters who came from Paris to Basel. Born in 1424 in Stein on the Rhine, on the Swiss-German border near Schaffhausen, he bore the appellation Von Stein (Latin, *a Lapide*) to denote provenience. As such he was widely known. Wimpheling calls him a Swabian, which would not be incorrect for the time. Although he was a Humanist of sorts, his chief interest lay in theology and Aristotelian philosophy. In the Nominalist-Realist controversy he stood out as a Realist, following what was known as the *via antiqua*. After preliminary studies in Leipzig and Louvain, he went to the University of Paris in 1454 to pursue theology, but at the same time taught philosophy. In 1464 he joined the theological faculty at the Sorbonne but left the same year for Basel, in order to get some Realists placed in the Humanistic faculty. His influence there was strong enough to secure him the deanship of the faculty—he was the first dean from the Realist camp—but after 1465 he does not seem to have played a very important role. Between 1467 and 1474 we find him in Paris again taking part in the establishment of the printing trade there. He had probably learned the trade from the printers Fust and Schäffer on a visit to Mainz. It was he who interested Amerbach in printing. In all likelihood Heynlin started the first press at the Sorbonne in 1470 and helped in preparing manuscripts for the press, making chapter divisions, summaries, and indices. He also directed Reuchlin, though a Nominalist, to Humanism, and similarly influenced Agricola. In 1469 he was honored with the rectorate of the University of Paris—a high distinction for one not even born on French soil, and a good example of the cosmopolitanism of the medieval world of scholarship. In 1472 he was awarded the degree of Doctor of Philosophy.

Heynlin has been classified among the early Humanists. His addresses contain evidence of this, although Humanism was not his primary goal. As a man and scholar he opposed arrogance, contentiousness and empty display of learning, and he did not share the Scholastic enthusiasm for logic and verbal virtuosity.

In 1474—perhaps late in 1473—Heynlin left Paris once more and became a preacher in Basel, Bern, and Baden. He felt that as a clergyman he could be more persuasively effective in spreading his Humanist-Realist views and reach a larger audience than he could as a professor. He spent most of the next four years in Basel, preaching in the St. Leonhard Church, and toward the end of his stay also in the cathedral. Returning to Basel for good in 1484, he preached in the cathedral until 1487 as canon. Later that year he entered the Carthusian monastery, where he died in 1496.

During all his years in Basel, Heynlin was the center of a learned group. It was chiefly he who shaped the ideas and ideals of the Humanists there, especially those of Brant. The latter's deep love for the Virgin Mary also stemmed from Heynlin, as did his predilection for Virgil. It was probably he who interested Brant in printing and got him started in it. But as Heynlin grew older, his Humanism was subordinated to ideas of Christian morality. It was Heynlin who made Brant conscious of the moral corruption he sensed all around him, and instilled in him the desire to turn society away from worldliness. This became an obsession with Brant.

Heynlin himself must finally have sensed the futility of this struggle, as did many of the Basel Humanists. He felt that truth was dying. This pessimism and a religious-philosophical dualism were among the chief reasons for his retiring from the world to the eternal silence of St. Bruno's disciples, the Carthusians. He once remarked that he "believed with St. Jerome that it is safer to be saved by oneself than to perish with many." Convinced that the wisdom of God seems folly to the learning of this world, he strove to show that worldly knowledge depends upon divine letters, and that it is the thoughtful man's duty to point this out to his fellow men. As for those in charge of the new invention of printing, he held it to be their duty to furnish men with the never-changing essentials of Christian welfare—the thoughts of the most profound thinkers.

These ideas made a deep impression upon young Brant, but no more so than did Heynlin's aversion to all philosophical specula-tion. Heynlin was first and foremost a preacher; following Cu-sanus, he restricted himself to practical morality and religiosity and, in a more limited sense, to Humanistic education. This should be borne in mind when Brant's *Narrenschiff* and his philosophy in general are appraised.

Heynlin was well acquainted also with Wimpheling and Trit-heim, and among his disciples in Basel was Geiler von Kaisers-berg, the famous preacher of Strasbourg. Peter Schott, Brant's old friend, had come in contact with him in Paris. But Brant was dear-est to his heart, as the only one who followed his thinking all the way.

Heynlin's Humanism, then, had its limitations. Being of an early date, so far as Germany was concerned, it was not yet directed at the esthetic beauty or the human content of the Classics. It turned to the ancient writers chiefly because they opened new horizons and, equally important, offered models of style worth imitating. Purification of style was a necessity because Scholasticism had well-nigh ruined the Latin style of the scholarly world in Germany. The image of a poet in the Germany of those days was that of a recluse poring over huge folios (still so depicted in some of the woodblocks of Brant's edition of Virgil from 1502), and the poet's subject matter was conceived as cribbed, cabined, and confined by the narrow vista of the times.

Of the early German Humanists, only Reuchlin had a vision of the deeper meaning of Humanism. Not until a second generation represented by Brant's pupil Jacob Locher, the author of the Latin version of the *Narrenschiff*, had grown up and matured, did a broader, more human concept of Humanism come generally into its own. But this new concept met with the vigorous disapproval of the older generation, represented especially by Wimpheling and Geiler, who thought that the cultivation of the Classics for their own sake was anti-Christian. As will be seen in Chapter 2, even Brant frowned on Locher's type of Humanism.

The policy of the Roman curia in the late fifteenth century was anything but liberal. Naturally its absolutism is reflected in the attitude of its stanch supporters among the Realists. We need not be surprised, then, that they did not dare deal constructively with the burning questions of the day in the field of Church politics. And, indeed, they would hardly have been able to do so effectively, even if they had wanted to. Their philosophy contended that so long as every man strives for the good, he can live under and tolerate almost any kind of regime. Consequently they hedged on many of the more important questions, while at the same time playing the role of stern judges in matters of individual morality. Each one set himself up as a judge in his own particular field of interest. Among other goals, Brant assigned himself the task of pointing out the sins, basic and secondary, as well as the peccadilloes of his contemporaries. Wimpheling berated priests who dallied with women. Tritheim, abbot of the Benedictine monastery of Sponheim after 1485, pressed for the revival of defunct monastic orders.

The Humanism of these men, especially Brant, will be discussed later. As for their relation to the Reformation, suffice it to say here that they sensed flaws, mostly in the lower echelons of the clergy, and strove to correct them. But in doing so they were bound to authority. Too often they acted like moral pedants.

On the other hand, surveying the more enduring, positive qualities of this Basel group, we come to the conclusion that teaching in the broadest sense was one of their paramount achievements. In this both Wimpheling and Brant excelled, the former with the help of his epoch-making educational tract *Adolescentia,* the latter in the lecture halls of the University of Basel and in his writings— especially the *Narrenschiff*—as well as in the printers' shops of the town. The two had much in common. In Strasbourg there are many letters (in copies) from Wimpheling to Brant, fewer from Brant to him. Indeed, Wimpheling often prods his lukewarm correspondent.

As for the chasm between the old Scholastic and the new Humanistic system of education, Brant was definitely on the side of the latter. He also enjoyed the reputation of being a good, stimulating teacher. His associations with students were informal and helpfully intimate. Teaching regularly in the divided Humanistic faculty, as well as in that of law, he showed them the way to the Latin Classics, as the students later attested with considerable enthusiasm. Most eloquent of these is Jacob Locher. In an epistle published as a preface to his *Narrenschiff* translation of 1497, Locher writes:

"I remember pleasantly that as a young lad in 1487 I earned the rewards of a happy academic life with you as my teacher. O sweet discussions which, graced by your delightful lectures, we enjoyed when you taught us in the public auditoriums. To our youthful ears, boisterous as we were because of our tender youth, you offered good and beneficent studies with your wonted eloquence. How often in the crowded classroom did you not call to life the contests of the poets and the sonorous songs of the ancients? How often did you not caress with loving murmur the Orphic and Delphic songs? How often did you not, with the skill of your Phoebus and your laurel that you deserve as a crown, draw me to the green pastures of Aganippe and to the gushing Castalian streams? Just as the prince of Attic eloquence, Demosthenes, the tender disciple of our Plato, was inspired by an oration that the most stirring orator Callistratos delivered from Oropos, just so you, beloved teacher, first led my mind to the happier retreats of study, to the more joyful grottos by your pleasant manner and urbanity. Therefore we do not hesitate to express to you not only the thanks we wish to give, but all the thanks our poor heart is capable of. For if I should try to pay you now for the eloquence you transmitted and for the inspiration of the muses, no eloquence of the pen and no thickness of Egyption papyrus could do justice to our sweat." [31]

This tribute by one not given to flattery, couched in a Latin not yet entirely free of Scholastic influence, speaks well for the Humanistic impact of Brant's teaching and his genuine enthusiasm for the Classics.

But Brant's academic position and activities, particularly as a teacher of the Humanities, do not emerge clearly from the university records still available in Basel. We know that Johann Mathias von Gengenbach taught "freie Künste" at the university as early as 1465 and, indeed, that the subject had been introduced there even sooner by Peter Luder. In August, 1470, Gengenbach's assignment was expanded to one hour a day of "arts" and one of "poesy." This he continued at least until 1480, so that he was definitely Brant's teacher. Then Von Gengenbach entered the faculty of law, which paid better and was not a stepchild, like the divided faculty of Humanities. He lectured on Virgil. But we hear nothing more of "poesy" until Jacob Carpentarius (Zimmermann) was appointed in 1489 to teach it. However, Locher's letter proves that he was a Latin student of Brant two years before. The answer seems to lie in the fact that there were three types of teacher: volunteer monks from the monasteries; laymen who had a tenuous academic standing as tutors and who usually taught in the "Burses" (this must have been Brant's position at first); and regular professors, always few in number, even in law.

Then in 1492 Diebold Westhofer (rector in 1506) was assigned to the Humanities, although he, a jurist, was incompetent in the field at that time and was given three years to prepare himself. Why Brant was not chosen in his stead is not clear, unless it be because he became dean of the law faculty at that very time. Yet apparently it was Brant who actually took charge in the Humanities after Von Gengenbach. In 1496 the official university "Erkenntnisbuch" (fol. 153b) notes negotiations between the university authorities and Brant with a view to his assuming the law professorship of Dr. Durlach and resuming "poesi . . . als er sich dess begeben hat" ("poesi . . . which he had given up").

As in the Classics, Brant was also strong as a teacher of law, especially in the recapitulation and exegesis of existing sources and writings, which required more reproductive than creative talents but could be accomplished by means of stimulating lectures and discussions.

The books written or edited by Brant during this time will later be discussed in more detail. For the present, a casual look at some of the works he compiled, edited, and published during these early years for the purposes of his teaching at the university may throw some light on the nature of that teaching. Important among these works is the comprehensive textbook of 1490, published by Furter, entitled *Expositiones sive declarationes omnium titulorum tam civilis quam canonici* ("Expositions or explanations of all divisions of law, civil as well as canon"). In the preface he stresses its usefulness and practical value for students. The work, which has some characteristics of a modern case book, proved so popular that edition after edition appeared over a period of many years, supplemented by annotations provided by the jurists Jacques Cujacius and Jean Wesembecs. If Brant's own commentary becomes sketchier toward the end, he blames this upon the *importunitas* of the printer, who eagerly pressed him to finish the manuscript.

New light is cast upon the work, as well as upon Brant's lectures on civil law at the university, by the Basel copy of the incunabulum *Apparatus Institutionum* (Basel: Wenssler, 1478—Hain's Catalog no. 9507)—that Brant used. Almost every page contains copious closely written notes (in ink) in his hand—comments, additions based upon his own experience, corrections, new punctuation, and underscoring. All of them point to his own *Expositiones sive declarationes*. . . . Even the arrangement of the topics in the two works indicates this close relationship.

In 1493 he edited the *Decretum Gratiani summo studio et cum libris Biblie accurate concordatum* ("The canonical rules of Gratianus carefully worked out and coordinated with the Bible"), which deals with canon law. In a prose epilogue, he praises the work as adding glory to Basel, "which is to be honored for its learning, letters, and printing." After having used them for a number of years, he edited and revised, in 1500, the lectures on law of

Jean Baptiste de Gasalupis, *De modo studendi in utroque iure* ("How to study both civil and canon law"), a practical text, also published by Furter, whose title has a modern ring.

Another type of activity in which Brant became engaged as early as the late 1470's, and which continued to occupy his attention for the remainder of his stay in Basel, is to be found in his role as an expert counsellor for some of the Basel printers and publishers. These printers, though well educated and trained for their profession, as has been noted, needed advisory experts to select manuscripts, edit them, establish reliable texts, and write letters or verses for the colophon, which recommends the book to the reader or dedicates it to some dignitary. Brant probably began this kind of work about the time he secured his baccalaureate degree in 1477, in all likelihood getting a start through his acquaintance with Bergmann, his fellow student, and through a recommendation by Heynlin, an expert in this field. Through the latter, too, he became acquainted with Amerbach. Work for the printers, which we found to be one of the more significant activities of Brant's career, led directly to the most important book from his pen, the *Narrenschiff*.

After the lapse of almost five hundred years, we have no way of determining how many books Brant helped edit, for some of the Basel works of the time omit all such indications. In general it may be said that he worked only on books that served his religious, moralistic-political ideals. He exercised a particularly strong influence on Bergmann, as the latter himself testifies in the letter to their fellow student Wymmar von Erkelenz, by then dean of the Aachen Church of the Virgin. The letter was published as a preface to the *Varia Carmina* of Brant.[32] But he was also in the employ of Amerbach, Furter, Froben, Petri, and others. It is believed that at least one-third of all books published in Basel during the decades when Brant lived there owe something to him. At the start he had to do much of the work anonymously. Under orders he prepared many a colophon without signing it. But even at an early date he appended his name when making a more or less important contribution, as in Tritheim's famous *De scriptoribus ecclesiasticis* ("On ecclesiastical writers"), 1494. This is a sort of encyclopedia, in which Brant himself is discussed. Here, too, he in turn contributed an appreciative notice on Reuchlin and also appended an eighteen-line distich. It will be discussed in Chapter 4. Other works to which he demonstrably gave help during this time are writings of St. Augustine (Amerbach, 1489) and St. Ambrose (Amerbach, 1493); the *Rhetorica Divina* of William, Bishop of Paris (Froben, 1492); and the *Historia Baetica* ("History of Guadalquivir, Spain") by Veradus (Bergmann, 1494).

From approximately the middle of the 1480's on, Brant, feeling the necessity of addressing the common people, too, started to cultivate writing in his German mother tongue. This was not easy because he had been trained exclusively in Latin and because there existed very little contemporaneous literature in the vernacular of any value for him as a model. But he considered it imperative to reach the masses, if he was to achieve his goals as a deeply religious, deeply patriotic moral-political publicist. Addressing the dignitaries of the Church and the temporal rulers from the Emperor down was desirable. But the people themselves had to be reached, too.

A special type of popular work Brant began editing during this earlier period of his life is represented by broadsides, first in Latin, then in German. Each was accompanied by one or several woodcuts designed to attract attention and to appeal to the illiterate, who, of course, were legion.[33] These broadsides, forerunners of the pamphlets so common during the Reformation era, usually dealt with some freak of nature or some remarkable occurrence in which Brant saw portents of events he feared would occur or which had already occurred. In this activity he became a precursor of the modern journalist and prepared the way for his *Narrenschiff*. But he did not himself make sketches for woodcuts, although he may have assisted the artists by giving them hints and instructions. Some of these verses, as well as longer works, involve Maximilian, who in 1486 became Roman King and in 1493 Emperor. Early examples are *Von dem donnerstein gefallen . . . vor Ensisheim* ("The meteor that fell . . . near Ensisheim" [1492]) and *Von der erlichen schlacht der Tutschen by Salyn* ("The honorable battle of the Germans at Salins" [1493]), both printed by Bergmann. But since the more significant references to Maximilian come in a later period, they will be discussed in succeeding chapters.

It is interesting to note how Brant trained himself as a writer in

German. He accomplished it by turning Latin into German, at first laboriously and awkwardly, but gradually with more facility and skill. His development can be traced by studying a series of translations from the Latin he essayed during these years for that express purpose. His Latin distich on the total eclipse of the sun on March 16, 1485, a weak effort in itself,

> Bis dedit octo dies forte et tot Martius horas:
> Versus ad occiduas sol tenebrosus aquas.

is turned into the following almost unintelligible German:

> Nach zehen sexs Mertz stund ouch tag
> Vil kleines schins die sun hie pflag,

More ambitious are five other such works, known as (1) *Ave præclara* ("Hail, illustrious one"), a ninety-five line hymn to Mary (one of several such poems), unfortunately not preserved exactly as Brant translated it; (2) a *Cato;* (3) a *Facetus;* (4) a *Moretus;* and (5) the *Thesmophagia* (or *Phagofacetus*).[34] The second, third, and fourth are general guides to human behavior, the last a treatise on good table manners. All five are in verse. Although in part printed after the *Narrenschiff* (the last four in the spirit of that work), they must have been written earlier. The first such attempt, the hymn to Mary, is a clumsy rendering clinging slavishly to the Latin and sometimes difficult to understand because of its clipped style. An example (ll. 5–9):

> Ein beschloszne porte   zu allen orten
> hast des vatters worte
> und die sonn der gerechtigkeit
> bekleit   und der menschheit
> geboren die warheit.

("A closed gate   in all places,/you have clothed [adorned] the Father's words/and the sun of justice/and have given   birth/to truth for mankind.")

Cato is hardly better (ll. 119–22):

Bistu allt und erzalst all zyt
Die werck und wort vil ander lüt,
Schaff das die tugent by dir ston
Die du in jugent hast gethon.

("If you are old and always tell/ Your works, and words to other people,/ See to it that virtue abides with you/ Which in youth you practiced.")

The *Facetus* is freer, introduces proverbs, of which Brant was very fond, and other original material, and seems more like an independent creation. The same is true of *Moretus*. From *Facetus* (ll. 293–96):

Nit wellest in eins andern ern
Mit diner sichlen schnyden kern,
Huet dich das du nit stossen wet
Din versen in eyns andern ee bet.

("Do not cut into another's honor/ With your sickle,/ And do not dig/your heels into another's marriage bed.")

In the *Thesmophagia,* finally, Brant has found himself as a versifier in the vernacular (ll. 707–12):

Bisz har sint wir mit synn unnd wort
Gesessen an des disches bort,
Nun kumbt die muosz unnd hoflich spiel,
Do mit so kurtzen wir die wil.
Der koch sich sehen laszt ouch dann,
Noch dem gelert ist haff unnd pfann . . .

("Up to now we have been/ At table with mind and word,/ Now follow leisure and polite play;/ Thus we pass the time./ The cook is seen soon after/ The dishes have been emptied . . .").

Here we are reminded of Chapter 110a in the second edition of the *Narrenschiff,* which now Brant was ready to launch. But the bulk of his writing was still in Latin and remained so for some time. Much of it was verse, and a good deal of that in honor of Mary. The language in each work depended upon the audience for which it was meant, as a part of his effort to reach that audience effectively.

In a recent monograph Wilfried Werner[35] has studied the passion and Easter plays in their transition from Latin to the vernacular. As in the case of the liturgical plays from the thirteenth century on, we find that in Brant's works, also, German gradually appears more often side by side with Latin. The balance shifts as he assumes ever more the role of one who would influence all the people. The latter are becoming more than a passive, massive agglomeration of members of the *sancta ecclesia* and the *imperium romanum*. They have emerged as human beings who want to experience the world—Church as well as Empire. As such they are entering into a new relationship with their environment; what happens there is linked with their own personal fate. This they realize for the first time. And so the change in language in Brant, who realizes it also, is not merely a matter of translation or adaptation of words; it signifies a change of the purpose to which the words are put. Consequently the tone and emphasis in the German as contrasted with the Latin works are quite different.

We may go even a step further. Both in Latin and in German there are different levels in Brant's language, from the straightforward declarative to the hypotactic, depending upon the type of material he is presenting.[36]

CHAPTER 2

Later Years in Basel and Strasbourg

I Literary Interests and Associates

ALL of Brant's writings preceding the *Narrenschiff*, even the Latin works, but especially those written in German, lead up to his masterpiece, which appeared in 1494. This is particularly true of the German broadsides, illustrated with woodcuts, and of the four aforementioned German works on behavior, *Cato, Facetus, Moretus,* and *Thesmophagia*. To be sure, some of the latter were printed later—*Facetus* and *Moretus* not until 1496—but internal evidence, as we found, suggests dates at least six years earlier. As has also been noted, these works have much in common. They are written in a language that has not yet shaken off the crudities of a dialectal vernacular tongue more subliterary than the language of the *Narrenschiff*. They are cast in the free four-beat verse pervading German literature of the time. The rhyming is comparatively pure, at least within the framework of the dialect; and the subject matter has topical interest, less to the upper class than to the high and low bourgeoisie.

This subject matter is a far cry from that of the polished courtly Middle High German classical literature of the twelfth and thirteenth centuries, which, as a product of knighthood, had become an anachronism. Consequently Brant and his contemporaries were forced to cast about for entirely new heroes and new subjects that would hold the attention of their contemporaries, especially the middle class.[1] Brant's search for a hero was solved by the appearance of Maximilian on the political scene.

In a sense Maximilian afforded him the type of leader he needed. After his election to the Roman kingship in 1486, which preceded his coronation as Emperor seven years later, he became Brant's idol, the noble ruler who would unite the princes and give new power, prestige, and peace to a resuscitated empire, ward off the French, and check the inroads of the Turks. Brant wrote two poems on Maximilian's election to the kingship. Again and again he hints, prods, and presses Maximilian to action, as in Verardi's *In laudem* . . . *Ferdinandi Hispaniorum regis* ("In praise . . . of the Spanish king Ferdinand" [Bergmann, 1494]) and in Ludwig Bebenburg's *Germanorum veterum principum zelus et fervor* ("The zeal and fervor of the German princes of old" [Bergmann, 1497]). Among broadsides of that type not yet mentioned are *Von der wunderbaren geburt des kindes bei Worms* ("Birth of a deformed child at Worms" [1495]), *Die wunderbare sau zu Landser im Sundgau* ("A deformed sow at Landser in the Sundgau" [1496]), *Von der zwifaltigen gans und der sau zu Gugenheim im Elsasz* ("The two-headed goose and the sow at Gugenheim in Alsace" [1496]); and the Latin *De inundatio Tybridis* ("The flood of the Tiber" [1495]), *De insigni cerva Regie maiestati donata* ("The unusual stag given to the Emperor" [1495]), and *Auspicii falconum . . . explanatio* ("Explanation of the portent of the hawks," [1495]).

Maximilian was a learned ruler who knew six languages and showed an interest in many sciences and arts, among them mathematics, history, poetry, architecture, music, and painting. His marriage to Bianca Sforza was a happy event that secured him a rich dowry.[2] Some of his military expeditions were successful. He drove the Hungarians out of Austria in 1490 and defeated the Turks in the Battle of Villach in 1492, and the French at Salins in 1493. He also checked the feuding princes through the Diet of Worms (1495) and established the Public Peace (Ewiger Landfrieden).

Unfortunately, however, he seemed to lack the *élan* needed to achieve the lofty goals he cherished and Brant dreamed of. Early in his career he was humiliated as a prisoner in Bruges (1488); let Charles VIII of France steal Anne of Brittany from him; and handed Basel and adjacent territories over to the Swiss and Milan to Louis XII. His attempt to establish political reforms in Germany, as well as his policies with regard to France, Switzerland, and the Ottoman Empire suffered shipwreck because he lacked initiative, had too many irons in the fire, was too sanguine, and failed to gain the support of his own nobles, with whom he often feuded. No wonder that Brant, though always remaining his loyal panegyrist, was in secret often his unhappy subject.

Maximilian grew to know Brant well and admire him. He probably first heard of him after his coronation.

Though disappointed in the Emperor, Brant did not give up his illusion of a strong unified German empire, leading the temporal Christian world to ever loftier heights. His patriotism was nourished by some of his teachers in Basel, but its strength was also due in a measure to the fact that he spent almost his entire life at outposts of Germanic civilization and enjoyed all of his education on Germanic soil.[3] Although not as narrowly nationalistic as modern patriotism tends to be, his patriotism shared some of its characteristics.

Another source of Brant's inspiration was the teaching of four men who may well have influenced him more than any others. One was his Basel teacher in canon law, Peter von Andlau; the second was Professor Hugonis; the third his confidant and mentor in Basel, Heynlin; and the fourth Geiler von Kaisersberg.

Peter von Andlau, already referred to, was a distinguished member of the community who helped found the university and served three times as dean and once as rector. Trained as a Scholasticist in Heidelberg, he became interested in Humanism in Pavia. In his writings[4] he insisted upon spotless lives for the clergy and their strict avoidance of interference in secular matters, as well as the establishment of a body of public law that would strengthen the temporal power.

Von Andlau's concept[5] of the Holy Roman Empire was a potent factor in shaping Brant's own views. He had absolute faith and complete confidence in the Empire, believed that its spiritual and temporal powers were divinely ordained (*ordinacione dei*) and that, since spiritual matters take precedence over temporal, the Pope, as the head of Christendom, can claim rank above the Emperor. The latter, however, is the highest temporal authority. When the dignity of the Roman *imperium* came into the hands of the Germans, he reasoned, this was a divine dispensation because of their magnanimity, nobility, and sincere love of the orthodox faith. If the Empire was showing signs of weakness, which he feared would cause its downfall, it was because of the laxity of manners and morals among the people and the failure of the nobles to rally around the Emperor, who was in a disadvantageous position in relation to the papacy. Von Andlau's rem-

edy was greater pride and patriotism on the part of all, and the
introduction of Roman law into Germany in an effort to bolster
the imperial power. But he didn't realize that he was only trying
to shore up a political anachronism.

Professor Hugonis has been mentioned as a Basel scholar whom
Brant served as *famulus*. His ideas about the Pope as the spiritual
ruler and supreme head of the Christian world, his supremacy
over the Emperor because of the latter's subordinate position as
a temporal ruler, and finally the hegemony of the German people
over all other nations, which imposes special obligations, strongly
presage Brant's later views.[6] That Hugonis was a Nominalist did
not seem to matter.

Heynlin's influence has already been discussed. He also instilled
in Brant the feeling that the age was morally decadent and in
need of thorough reform. This included not only the eradication
of cardinal sins, but also of minor vices, peccadillos, and even
foibles, all of which are unsightly in God's eyes and weaken the
Empire spiritually and temporally.

Sins, follies, and foibles are visited upon man, not to punish
him, but to put him to the acid test of his virtue, Heynlin insisted.
Since the Germans are the God-chosen leaders of Christianity,
their superiority carries with it unique obligations, as Hugonis,
too, believed. Ultimately Heynlin himself despaired of achieving
these goals, either as a university teacher in Paris or Basel, or as
a preacher in Bern[7] and elsewhere. So he retired from the world.
But he hoped Brant would be more successful by reaching the
common people as well as the upper classes in their own tongue
and at their own level of understanding through the printing press
and the woodcut.

Brant adopted Heynlin's views. Whereas his *Narrenschiff* ap-
peals with this line of reasoning to all classes, including the
masses, such a poem as "De corrupto ordine vivendi pereuntibus"
("On those perishing because of the corruption of orderly life"
[1498]), the subtitle of which states that lack of order has been
the cause for the destruction of things, reflects Heynlin's and
even more Von Andlau's philosophy. Both show Italian influence,
especially that of Thomas of Aquinas. Such lines as these occur
in Brant's poem: *Ordo est qui parvos tollit in astra lares* ("It is
order that raises the little things in life to the stars"), and *Ordine*

perverso, nil placet usque Deo ("When order is subverted, nothing pleases God").

That Brant praises Heynlin and holds him up as an example in his *Narrenschiff*—for him no usual means of personal allusion—indicates his high regard for his idol and is further proof of Heynlin's influence upon the work. I quote four passages: Chapter 41, 11. 5–12:

> Therefore those men enjoy renown
> Who spurn the world and on it frown
> And walk through valley, over hills,
> To shun the world's rebuff and ills,
> Avoiding guilt where'er they go,
> And yet they suffer many a blow:
> The world does not deserve one whit
> That such good men inhabit it.[8]

In Chapter 105, 11.17–22, Brant alludes more pointedly to him:

> When fools a good man see who seeks
> To do what's right but never speaks,
> They say: "A bigot is this man,
> He'd fain be a Carthusian!
> Hypocrisy is that man's share,
> And in our Lord he would despair." [9]

Noteworthy in particular is the allusion to the eternal silence imposed upon the Carthusians. Again, 11. 43–50:

> "If just like this man everyone
> Should put Carthusian garments on
> Who would increase the population
> And give men wisdom, information?
> Of God's desire he makes abuse
> Who treats himself like this recluse
> And thinks but of himself alone.
> Such incantations fools intone." [10]

Finally lines 61–64:

> Say that I had two souls in me,
> To fools I'd give the one soul free,

> But since I have one soul alone,
> There's need for me to guard the one.[11]

This last is virtually a direct quotation from Heynlin himself, who is said to have remarked to Junker Brandolf von Stein, one of his critics: "If he had two souls, he would have been satisfied to risk one of them to a life of jollification" ("Wann er zwo seelen hätte, wollte er gnug die eine an gut Gesellen gewagt han").[12]

It is little wonder, then, that when Heynlin lay on his deathbed in 1496, Brant was the only outsider permitted to visit him. One of the comparatively few poems Brant wrote with his heart's blood is an epigram on Heynlin's death: "Father Lapide," he exclaims, "what happier and more joyful fate could ever/have befallen you/than that, after so much time spent in our fraudulent age/and such grave tribulations, you now joyfully approach the stars!/ Present as I was when you died, I heard that you/ had no fear of death or of the fateful day/ . . . As God gave you hours of quiet while you lived,/ He will give you even better ones among those who dwell above/ . . . I shall be stirred to bear testimony for you on Judgment Day/how you embraced death with ready willingness./ I pray to you, worthy father now in heaven,/ remember your wretched little son./ May glory, everlasting life, well-being, good name, joy and happy rest be yours, as you deserve." [13]

An offer by Brant to erect a monument in Heynlin's honor on the grounds of the monastery was turned down by Prior Lauber, much to Brant's disappointment.

The relationship of Geiler and Brant is somewhat different. Although Geiler, born in Schaffhausen, was about twelve years older than Brant, they seem to have influenced each other. In 1471 Geiler had come from Freiburg to Basel to continue his studies of theology, and remained there until 1476, serving as dean of the Humanistic faculty in 1474 and securing his license and doctorate in theology in 1475. Consequently he spent about a year there with Brant. As already noted, he went to Strasbourg as a preacher in 1478.[14]

Geiler's sermons, even those delivered before the publication of the *Narrenschiff* in 1494, some of which Brant undoubtedly heard, show remarkable resemblance to that work. Geiler is a defender of the Church, a moral reformer and, like Heynlin, opposed to speculative philosophy in religious matters. He attacks not only sins like adultery, but also follies and foibles like vanity, love of luxury and pleasure, and disregard of the Sabbath. He would awaken man's conscience and lead him back to God; and he warns men to prepare now for the hereafter before it is too late. He preaches in the homely Alsatian dialect of the people and defends the use of the mother tongue against the Humanists, even coining words when he can find no equivalents for the Latin (*Grüssbarkeit* for *affabilitas*).[15] He uses fables and proverb after proverb for illustrative purposes, as well as witty sayings to brighten his teachings: "*anima,* zuvor hies sie *sel,* nun hat sie das *e* von der Eva genommen, das sie *esel* heisst." ("*anima,* formerly it was called soul [*sel*], now it took the *e* from Eve, so that it is now ass [*esel*].") Or: "Wir heissen alle *doctores,* wir seind aber nur halbe *doctores:* das mittel theil thor: doc, tor, res; den anfang und das end haben wir nit."[16] ("We are all called *doctores,* we are however only half *doctores:* the middle part [tor] fool: doc, tor, res; the beginning and the end we do not have.")

If any single quality stands out in Geiler's sermons, it is his flair for the rules of rhetoric according to pseudo-Ciceronian principles. The same attribute, we will find, is an integral characteristic of the *Narrenschiff.*

So much for the impact of Geiler's sermons on Brant. Less than four years after the appearance of the *Narrenschiff,* Geiler, on the other hand, began to preach on the individual chapters of the work and continued doing so for a year and a quarter, with brief respites only when he was away from his pulpit.

In the *Varia Carmina* Brant pays Geiler a fine tribute: "You are my teacher, my father, and master,/you, the glory, fame, and adornment of our fatherland./ Our mother Strasbourg glows with your teaching/. . . A multitude of people follow you, your reputation/is excellent, you are the father and the salvation of the people./ May the good Lord grant you such a life/as you prepare for all the people in word and deed."[17] Brant also composed a poem on the occasion of Geiler's death in 1510. The first four lines, slightly modified, became the famous preacher's epitaph: "He whom the city of Strasbourg deservedly laments,

Johannes/ Geiler, whose home is the mountain of Caesar—
Kaisersberg—:/under this site you lie, which you erected as
the faithful priest,/teaching beneficent words for almost six
quinquennia."[18]

Brant himself made a German translation of this poem. The
pertinent lines read:

> Den alles stroszburg weint billich,
> Johannes geiler lobes Rich,
> Den doctor Keisersberg man nant,
> Um den trurt warlich doctor brant,
> Das er gestorben ist in zyt.
> Hie under disem stul er lyt,
> Den er ob dreissig iaren hadt
> Regiert wol in predigers stadt.

Peter von Andlau, Hugonis, Heynlin, and Geiler, then, played
prominent roles in shaping the line of reasoning that Brant followed when he planned his *Narrenschiff* and an even more ambitious Latin work to be discussed presently. The high hopes
Brant placed in Maximilian served to buttress that thinking. One
additional factor helping to explain the temper of the *Narrenschiff*
is that mental attitude mentioned in Chapter 1, which grew from
his prudish, testy, critical disposition. He was impatient of way-
wardness and folly in any form, and he was meddlesome. Anyone
who irritated him, like the writer of the anonymous letter quoted
in Chapter 1, was likely to incur his wrath and to be branded
Nar, Nar, Nar. Thus the citizens of Bruges, who, as has been
noted, took Maximilian prisoner in 1488, were threatened by
Brant with destruction and extirpation for their perfidy and
sacrilege.[19]

It is natural that such a man should be given to satire. And
satire as well as panegyric is a natural mode of expression in an
age like Brant's when writers are casting about for new subject
matter. In satire, as will be seen, his teachers were Horace, Persius, and Juvenal.

So much for the intellectual background, beliefs, and emo-
tional qualities of the author who through broadsides and translations of treatises on manners prepared himself to write the
Narrenschiff, and who was encouraged by his friend Bergmann,

newly established as a printer, to proceed with this work and with the one that followed it in 1495. The literary antecedents and genesis of the *Narrenschiff* will be discussed in due time. Suffice it to say that within less than a generation it earned Brant an international reputation, renderings or adaptations in five languages appearing in fairly rapid succession.

II *Final Years in Basel*

During the last decade of the century, after Brant had received his doctorate, he was occupied with lecturing, teaching, and administering at the university. He also practiced law, acted as literary and technical adviser to Basel publishers, and studied intensively, especially in the library of the Carthusian monastery. Occasionally he also carried out missions for the bishop of Basel. By 1494 he was considered a celebrity. At the time of the Diet of Freiburg in that year, some delegates, among them Heinrich von Büno (or Bünau), the ambassador of the Elector of Saxony, and Johannes Wolf von Hermannsgrün from Magdeburg, a friend of Reuchlin, came to Basel expressly to pay him homage. It is therefore surprising that Brant found as much time for writing as he did.

One year after the appearance of the first edition of the *Narrenschiff* and two years before Locher's Latin version of it, Brant published one of his most ambitious works, again printed by Bergmann. Written in Latin prose, it bears the title *De origine et conversatione bonorum Regum et laude Civitatis Hierosolymae: cum exhortatione eiusdem recuperandae* ("On the origin and conversion of good kings and in praise of the state of Jerusalem: with an exhortation to reconquer it"). It was meant for the learned classes. As a literary achievement it is comparable to the *Narrenschiff*, but it is much more esoteric in style and content. Consequently it neither attained popularity nor reached wider circles of readers. Chapter 99 of the *Narrenschiff*, written with more feeling than any other chapter, may be considered as a brief treatment of the same theme on the popular level. It will be discussed in more detail.

It was stated that as early as 1494 Brant published a collection of Latin verse chiefly in honor of the Virgin Mary, and in 1498 he published an expanded edition under the caption *Varia Car-*

mina (Bergmann), including many nonreligious poems. Three editions appeared that year, one, by Grüninger (or Grieninger) in Strasbourg, unauthorized. While these poems are uneven in quality, some, like those on Heynlin's death and the one to Geiler, are noteworthy. Others, such as the one referred to above, on orderliness and the lack of it, throw light upon his philosophy. They will be discussed together with his other works in Chapter 6, Section I. In some poems we find him performing service as an editor. During each year he saw at least one work appear that bore the impress of his labors, the *Narrenschiff*, 1494; the work on Jerusalem, 1495; and (as editor) an important contribution to the Latin works of Petrarch, 1496 (Amerbach); the volume of Lupold Bebenburg already mentioned, 1497 (Bergmann); the *Revelations* of St. Methodius, 1498 (Furter); the *Panormia* of Ivo of Chartres, 1499 (Furter); and Gazalupis' *De modo studendi* . . . , 1500 (Furter).

One work, however, sometimes ascribed to Brant and his student Locher, was not by them. This is the first German translation of all the extant plays of Terence (Grüninger, 1499). It was Max Herrmann who in 1914 suggested cautiously that Brant and Locher may have been the authors.[20] Writers after 1914, for example, Josef Nadler, in his *Literaturgeschichte der deutschen Schweiz*,[21] accepted this mere hypothesis as a fact. But Herrmann's conjecture has now been refuted by Wolfgang F. Michael,[22] who shows that this edition of Terence contains errors that both Brant and Locher, who was an important figure in the development of the Humanist drama, could not have made.

The last years of the fifteenth century were stormy ones in Switzerland. Emperor Maximilian, anxious to incorporate the cantons in the Swabian league of estates, sent detachment after detachment of troops to chastise the Swiss for their stubborn unwillingness to join the league. He finally realized the hopelessness of his endeavors to persuade or force them, and in 1499, after his defeat at Dorneck, made peace with them in Basel. Soon after that, Basel, together with other towns, defected from the Empire and joined the Swiss Confederation. From that time on all of Switzerland at least informally severed its ties with the Empire. This, but especially the loss of Basel, proved a cruel blow to Brant, the ardent admirer of Maximilian and imperial patriot, who was always dreaming of expansion of the Empire, but never of its diminution.

Writers disagree as to whether Basel's transfer of allegiance played an important part in Brant's decision to turn his back upon that city, which had been his home for so many years. There may have been a combination of reasons, including the town's shift of allegiance, Brant's wish to escape his manifold duties in Basel, some of which he found irksome;[23] and his desire to return to Strasbourg, where his mother and several other relatives, as well as many friends, were still living. Certainly an honorable position awaited him—that of legal adviser of the municipal government. Moreover, by visits and correspondence he had always maintained good personal relations with prominent Strasbourgers. On the other hand, Basel later showed him no ill will for having left. When he returned in 1511 to settle the estate of his father-in-law, he was showered with honors as a "patron of the cause of letters." [24]

III *The Years in Strasbourg*

The post of Strasbourg legal adviser had been held for some time by one with the highest academic degree in law, the doctorate. So when it became vacant in 1500, Brant's friend and former associate at Basel, Geiler von Kaisersberg, called the attention of the municipal authorities to Brant as a promising candidate. To the official, Bechtold Offenburg, Geiler wrote as follows: "I have been informed that the city intends to appoint another doctor. I have thought of Dr. Brand [*sic!*], a child of the town and famous in all countries beyond other men. His writings show his knowledge in German and Latin. He could also for an hour each day read to the burghers' sons—information they would have to pay for dearly in foreign countries. All of this would be for a single remuneration. It also seems to me fitting that the city should have such a man from among its burghers, born here, and not a stranger. Such a man could better be relied upon. If you deem it good, this might be conveyed to others beside yourself. —Johann Kaisersberg." [25]

At the same time Geiler and other Strasbourg friends prevailed upon Brant to apply in person to the city council for the position.

So after the middle of January, 1500, shortly before the day of
the very saint for whom he was named, St. Sebastian (January
20), Brant dispatched a long letter to the Strasbourg council.
Among other things he wrote: "Recently [late in 1499] while on
a mission for the bishop of Basel, my gracious lord, when I spent
also a short time in your city of Strasbourg with my mother and
brothers, the news came to me from several gentlemen and pa-
trons that you have hitherto had a *doctor* whose advice was used
at proper times in legal matters and disputes, and who has
now taken and received leave from you. Wherefore I shall venture
to apply to you to ascertain whether in your prudence you might
accept and appoint me. I have thought further about this matter,
in view of the fact that I am a child of your honored city of
Strasbourg and still have there my mother,[26] brothers, and many
native and well-disposed gentlemen and friends. . . . I have
taken to heart the dictum of imperial law: *patria sua unicuique
debet esse charissima,* his own fatherland should be dearest to
everyone. The same love (as the poet says) attracts all people
and should not be forgotten. . . . Should you in your wisdom
desire to appoint another *Doctor,* and if you have not provided
yourselves with one yet, and if I may, in such highest endeavor,
serve you with obedient and friendly will as my gracious lords
and masters, preferring to attend you rather than princes or other
masters or cities, I hope you will pay heed to this letter of mine
with graciousness and favor." [27]

On August 17, 1500, the Strasbourg city council voted that
Brant was to be placed on the payroll beginning with the day
of his arrival and assumption of his duties. On January 13, 1501,
six months to the day before Basel formally joined the Swiss
Confederation, he was officially sworn in. Three years later, upon
the retirement of Johann Münch of Schlettstadt, he was promoted
to the post of municipal secretary ("Stadtschreiber"). He liked
to refer to himself as chancellor and later as arch-chancellor. On
his tombstone he is designated as *archigrammateus.*

The appointment was a happy one both for Brant and his native
town,[28] although it ended his university activities and his collaboration with the Basel publishers. But it did not curtail his writing,
in spite of his numerous duties as counselor of the magistrature,

editor of council minutes, transactions, resolutions, and official correspondence, censor, as well as liaison officer to keep the judicial branch posted on new statutes.

Historian and jurist that he was, the environment in which he worked in Strasbourg proved congenial. The constitution of the sovereign city-state had developed in a peculiar manner and occasionally not without violent upheavals. Its genesis was traceable to one of the earliest periods of the development of Germanic jurisprudence. In the archives Brant could find evidence of this, which fascinated him as a student of legislative history. It is no wonder then that he delved into these, in part, ancient documents with enthusiasm. He devoted much time during the first years organizing and classifying the archives. This task he performed so well that his successors had only to follow in his footsteps.

Because of the geographical location of Strasbourg, its importance as a free imperial city, its excellent administrative and public-safety program, and not least important, its industrial and economic prosperity, the city played a decisive role in matters affecting southwest Germany. Brant occupied an important position in all events affecting Strasbourg during his tenure of office, especially those in the field of law and jurisprudence. His name appears frequently in the documents of the time. Occasionally, with the permission of the council, he was involved as counsel in private litigation, as for instance in 1502 in a case of the canons of the cathedral against the lord of Weiersheim.

Brant won the confidence of his fellow citizens in a comparatively short time. The magistracy often complimented him upon his wise conduct of affairs and showed their appreciation. When he prepared a report in 1502 for the Emperor on measures to be employed in the case of suicides, the magistracy gave him a gratuity of fifty gold gulden, which would now be the equivalent of several hundred dollars. Besides, he received each year a gift of twenty gulden and a half-measure (Fuder) of wine.

In the political correspondence of the city,[29] the municipal archives, and the archives of the St. Thomas Church, there is abundant evidence of Brant's activity, official and unofficial. For instance, he wrote a report on the rules about ecclesiastical prebends and another on the escape of serfs. There is a long letter and a poem to him by a Benedictine monk against the opponents of immaculate conception, and other material on this problem, to be discussed later in this chapter. Sometimes, too, he commented on or annotated municipal documents, his contributions being recognizable only by his handwriting.

Occasionally he became guilty of that captious and testy manner that characterizes him as the author of the *Narrenschiff*. The annals he kept record the council's reprimand that "the municipal secretary shall not speak on matters or in decisions, except when he is asked." [30] But he never complained about such censure and usually maintained his dignity as the outstanding scholar and mainstay of the municipal government. When Brant complained to the councilmen that the *ammeister* had made pointed remarks aimed at him, he was told "to call upon him, talk to him in a friendly way, and be calm." [31]

Honors were bestowed upon him too. Emperor Maximilian, whom, as was noted, Brant idolized and often eulogized, summoned him to Innsbruck in 1502 as a consultant. Subsequently he appointed his "dear, loyal Sebastian Branndt" counselor and Count Palatine for services rendered. When the imperial letter pertaining to the former honor was read in a council meeting, Brant was forthwith given permission to pay Maximilian a visit, accompanied by a servant. On a second occasion, in 1508, Maximilian summoned him for confidential advice in a dispute with the city of Venice. Still another imperial summons, the purpose of which is shrouded in mystery, came in 1513.

Maximilian did not show lasting disfavor to either the town or to Brant when in 1501, and again in 1502 and 1504, Brant's friend Cardinal Raimund von Gurck, the papal legate, went on a mission not authorized by the Emperor, to collect indulgences in Strasbourg for combating infidels. On the contrary, he stipulated in 1505 that without the *ammeister's* consent neither an ecclesiastical nor a temporal court could sequester a Strasbourger's property. In 1508 he conferred on Strasbourg the privilege of minting gold coins. And when in 1512 a resolution of the imperial diet in Cologne threatened to curtail important privileges of the cities, Brant pleaded the case of Strasbourg before the Emperor, presenting him at the same time with a prize hunting falcon, and won his point. The Emperor's admiration for Brant, whom he promised an annual stipend of fifty gulden[32] and also appointed assessor of the imperial cameral court, was clearly the reason for such favors, although he never responded to Brant's persistent pleas for a crusade against the Turks. Nor was Maximilian the only potentate to honor Brant. The Elector of Mainz appointed him a member of his advisory council.

Prominent men wrote to him during these years. On April 7, 1507, Konrad Peutinger, the Augsburg Humanist, reported to him on his journey to India; and on August 20, 1513, Willibald Pirckheimer wrote from Nuremberg praising Brant's writings.

Brant also took an active part in establishing and administering poorhouses and hospitals in which persons with communicable diseases could be isolated. Since the city itself had no funds for this purpose, he joined members of the council in raising the necessary money. He also helped to prevail upon the council to provide fuel and kindling wood for these institutions.

Some of the principal works published by Brant during the later years of his residence in Basel have been mentioned. It has also been pointed out that his career as a writer and publicist did not come to an end when he left Basel. Indeed, the bibliography Schmidt offers indicates over thirty works either written, edited, or in some way supplemented by him after 1500. Some of these are of considerable importance, e.g., *Bischoff von Hoensteins waal* ("Election of the Bishop von Hoenstein" [1506–1507]), the *Freiheitstafel* ("Tablet of freedom" [after 1501]), the *Layen Spiegel* ("Layman's mirror" [1509]), and the *Clagspiegel* ("Mirror of lawsuits" [1516]), and an encomium of Emperor Maximilian (1520), in addition to over seventy epigrams. All of these will be discussed in Chapter 6. He continued writing occasional verse too. Strasbourg publishers now usually printed his works, among them Wehinger, Grüninger, Hupfuff, and Knoblouch.

In Basel, Brant had always quietly but consistently advocated the study of the Classics. Indeed it may be said that with his departure the first Humanistic era in Basel came to an end. In Strasbourg he continued this advocacy, and during the early years there he was somewhat of a pioneer in this respect. His editions of Aesop (1501) and Virgil (1502) illustrate this activity. As a friend of the Classics he also pressed the city council to establish a good public school. Wimpheling's decision to stay in Strasbourg for some time early in the century may have been influenced by

Brant. However, he did not maintain close relations with the younger generation of Humanists, such as Locher and Heinrich Bebel.

It has been noted that as early as 1494 Brant published a small volume of poems and in 1498 an expanded volume. One of the theses of his work to and about the Virgin is the assertion of his belief in the immaculate conception. In the fifteenth and sixteenth centuries, the immaculate conception was still a moot question in some quarters, though rapidly gaining favor. Brant felt bound to advocate and defend it with extreme vehemence. He added an ode to a poem of Wimpheling on the subject (1494), and in one of his own longer poems[33] went to extremes in defending it, using what he thought were analogies to prove his point. "The unique phoenix bird," he argues, "is reborn in fire, and so the unique Virgin provides life to the wretched. The Spanish tree gives forth winged birds. Who would deny that a virgin can give birth without man? . . ."[34] And in another poem against skeptics or *maculists,* as he calls them, dedicated to Dean Adelbert von Rotberg of Basel, he waxes so harsh that he excuses himself for being "carried away on a ship of fools" (*insana me modo nave vehi*).[35] In 1499, in his edition of the decrees of the Church Council of Basel, he reaffirmed faith in the doctrine.

Brant was censured in some quarters for his undue acerbity in this matter. Adam Werner von Temar in Heidelberg was among those who protested in 1502. But when a controversy erupted between a scurrilous Dominican monk, Wigand Wirt, a Thomist, who disputed the immaculate conception, and a Frankfurt priest of the Franciscan order, Hans Sprenger, the matter was left to Thomas Wolf, the Older (the uncle of an Alsatian Humanist by the same name),[36] and also to Brant himself to mediate the case. Wigand was declared in error, and neither his appeal to Pope Alexander VI in Rome, which involved two cardinals in the dispute, nor a sacrilegious Dominican plot that brought death by fire to four of the plotters in Bern in 1509, could change the decision.[37] After suffering many indignities, Brant was vindicated and his reputation enhanced when in Heidelberg in 1513 [38] Wirt finally recanted publicly under pressure and openly retracted any and all of his disparaging remarks against Brant, Wolf, and Wimpheling. Throughout this most unpleasant, long drawn-out affair Brant showed reserve and self-control, and a maturity he had rarely possessed during his earlier years.

He was cautious in a quarrel in 1505 between the Freiburg professors Zasius and Locher. Siding with Zasius, he succeeded, however, in keeping out of print the Latin-Greek epigrams against Locher which he contributed to Zasius' delight. "You [he addresses Locher, whose Latin name was Philomusus] will no longer be called Philomusus, but φιλομυνθος, or better Philomerda [lover of dung]." [39] Knowing the quarrelsome, vindictive nature of Locher, whom he was now ashamed to acknowledge as his pupil, he was well advised in keeping him in the dark concerning any involvement in the dispute. Consequently Locher always remained well disposed toward him.

Locher, a Swabian by birth, was fourteen years younger than Brant. It has been noted that he bestowed high praise upon his Basel teacher in the Humanities, especially Latin. In 1488 he matriculated in Freiburg, where Maximilian crowned him poet in 1497, the year in which he translated the *Narrenschiff*. Because of his quarrelsomeness he lost a professorship of poetry in Ingolstadt and, in 1506, a similar post in Freiburg, where he became involved in a dispute with Zasius. A poem he wrote that year on the Muses incurred the wrath of the older, more conservative Humanists, who found pagan sentiments in it. Most of the rest of his life was spent in Ingolstadt.

Though remembered primarily for his Latin version of the *Narrenschiff*, Locher deserves credit also as one of the first German Humanists to appreciate the ancient Classics for their own sake, an appreciation not shared by the older Humanists. His edition of Horace (1498) was the first to appear in Germany. Locher also had a gift for lyricism that Brant lacked. He was an avowed enemy of Scholasticism, also a central figure in the development of the Humanist drama. Indeed he initiated it in 1495 with his *Historia de Rege Franciae* ("History of the King of France"), performed in a garden of the University of Freiburg. [40]

Brant always remained a stanch defender of the Catholic faith. To that end he strove for the reform of morals among the priesthood, as Von Andlau and Wimpheling had done. With relatives and others he donated an altar to the Virgin Mary and various saints in the parish church of St. Martin. The theatrical performances he arranged or sponsored had a moral-didactic purpose. He wrote a Latin play on Hercules, now lost.[41]

One post that devolved upon Brant as chancellor of the Strasbourg city council, sometimes overlooked, is that of censor of publications. It led occasionally to embarrassing situations. In 1510 he had to proscribe Wimpheling's tract on education, *Diatriba*, because of its hostility toward the Dominicans and monks in general.

Also disconcerting was a conflict with Thomas Murner. One of the more prolific writers of his time, Murner, after supporting Luther for a while, became his bitter enemy and in Reformation caricatures was depicted as the "purring fool" (*Murr-Narr*), and as a brash, outspoken Franciscan. In several of his works he is deeply indebted to Brant.

After Wimpheling had written his *Germania* in 1501 to disprove the French claims to Alsace and to maintain that it had always been German, Murner published some sharp verse against his fellow Alsatian. In this connection Murner is mentioned for the first time in the minutes of the Strasbourg council in 1502. According to the entry, the printer of the poem was required to take an oath not to sell any more copies on pain of severe punishment.

The Emperor himself played a role in this matter. Partly through pressure applied by him, a municipal decree was issued in Strasbourg in the spring of 1504 prohibiting the publication of anything prejudicial "to the Pope, the king, this city or any other city, or to individuals, too, without the permission of the master [the *ammeister*, or mayor] and the council." [42] This did not impair Murner's standing with Maximilian; and in 1505 he was crowned poet laureate.

In 1517 Murner finished one of his principal works, *Die Gäuchmatt* ("The Fools' Meadow"), a satire on men who let women make fools of them. He sold the manuscript to the Strasbourg publisher Hupfuff for four florins. Hupfuff dutifully submitted the manuscript to the city council for censorship. We do not know Brant's personal reaction to the work as censor, but may guess that it was unfavorable. The *ammeister* discovered passages in it that displeased him, and two councilmen to whom Brant was instructed to show the manuscript found objectionable references to the Emperor, the house of Austria, and the Swiss. Informed of the council's disapproval, Murner wrote to Brant asking for the manuscript.[43] This seems to have helped to expedite its return. The manuscript went back to Hupfuff with an express warning that it was not to be printed in Strasbourg. Two years later, in 1519, Petri published *Die Gäuchmatt* in Basel.

The Zasius-Locher dispute made it clear that Brant did not become lightheartedly involved in controversies. Sometimes he simply ignored disputes or alluded to them only in a veiled way. This applies to the threat posed by Luther and his followers. Shortly before Brant's death, however, Murner accused him of negligence in his attitude as censor toward the enemies of Catholicism. We saw that he remained silent in the famous quarrel between Reuchlin and the Cologne Dominicans, in spite of Reuchlin's repeated efforts to implicate him.[44]

Around the turn of the century, at the very time Brant settled in Strasbourg, Wimpheling had founded a literary society there on the pattern of similar societies in Mainz, Vienna, and Schlettstadt. It was organized like a guild but also included clerical members, and aimed at cooperative endeavor among literary men. It also facilitated communication among writers who lived in different places and encouraged scholars to criticize each other's works. Visiting colleagues were sometimes honored and even boarded as the society's guests.

Brant was a co-founder and prominent member of this society. When in August, 1514, Erasmus, on his way from England to Basel, stopped at Strasbourg, he was graciously received and tendered a dinner by the members. After this visit Erasmus wrote a cordial letter to Wimpheling, praised "the incomparable Brant," and expressed his satisfaction at having embraced him.[45] Later, in a poem, he honored Brant by saying that while others enjoy the luster of their environment, Brant adds new glory to his native town. Erasmus founded a similar society in Basel. It is possible that on Brant's last journey in 1520, when he paid homage to Charles V in Ghent, he met Erasmus again. In spite of the fact, however, that both Brant and Erasmus corresponded with many famous Humanists of their day,[46] they seem never to have written to each other. Brant did, however, compose an epigram on the appearance of Erasmus' *Praise of Folly*. He thought this work would stir up more excitement than his *Narrenschiff*, because it attacks the upper class.

On January 12, 1519, Emperor Maximilian died, some three months before completing his sixtieth year. This was a severe loss to the city of Strasbourg, but an even harsher blow to Brant. As we have seen, Brant was disappointed in the ruler more than once, especially with regard to political matters. Many hopes had remained unfulfilled; many things had turned out differently from what he had expected. However, these disappointments were now dismissed and replaced by new hopes that under Maximilian's grandson and successor, Charles V, the ailing body politic would be given a new lease on life.

Brant himself was in ill-health during much of 1519, but in June of the following year he felt strong enough to join a delegation instructed by the city fathers to journey to Ghent, where the new ruler was holding court, ready to receive the homage of the Strasbourg citizenry. Early the same year Brant, with the help of several councilmen, had prepared a complete catalogue of all the rights and privileges granted over the years by the German emperors to the city. To these he now added some new immunities that it was hoped the Emperor might decree. At the same time, Pope Leo X was to be asked to reaffirm previous commitments to the town and to forbid the cumulation of benefices, which was regarded an evil.

Onuphrius accompanied his father on the journey to Ghent, which lasted from June to August. In Ghent Brant delivered a congratulatory address to Charles in Latin. The latter proved gracious, offering his hand to the delegation when they arrived and again as they left. Through his speaker, the governor of Burgundy, he pledged protection and good will.

The delegation also paid homage to the Emperor's brother, the Archduke Ferdinand, who gave them his word that he would always intercede on their behalf. In return for this, the Strasbourgers vowed renewed allegiance to the Emperor and Reich. On this journey Dürer made his portrait of Brant.[47]

August found Brant back in Strasbourg. In his *Annals* he reports: "From that time [June, 1520] to Simphor. [late in August] I was away, sent to Ghent to His Imperial Majesty. I returned in good health and safely, having attained the thanks of the Emperor for our congratulations. Praise to God on high." [48] About three months later, it seems, Brant penned what may have been his last letter (preserved in the St. Thomas archives). It was written November 16 to the dean of the St. Thomas chapter and recommended a boy for the choir.

During the last nine months of his life, a deep pessimism, nourished by congenital irritability and a nervous breakdown, held Brant in its grip. He realized that efforts to correct the many evils that had crept into the Church had been in vain. He was disturbed by the lack of cohesion everywhere evident in the Empire, and by the threat against the old hierarchy posed by the expanding religious schism. Finally he was apprehensive of the Turkish menace. As a result he feared a catastrophe of great magnitude. Alluding to a prophesy of Johann Stoffler, a Tübingen mathematician, that the year 1524 would witness a calamitous deluge, he warns: "Such confusion will arise everywhere,/such horrible happenings,/as though the whole world were to be destroyed./ May God help holy Christianity!/ O priesthood, let that warning be given to you,/so that you may not be devoured, destroyed./ May God will it that no deluge will come/that will devour the whole earth,/all of it, or scatter hordes of heathens/among all Christianity/who could destroy/the Christians completely . . . but as men act on earth,/given to vice, sin, disgraceful behavior—/take care that things don't get worse./ Without doubt great changes will occur/ in high and low, old and young,/in fruit, fish, birds, beast, and men . . ." [49]

The poem from which these lines are quoted was probably the last he ever wrote. Its pessimism contrasts sharply with the optimism expressed by Ulrich von Hutten to Pirckheimer on October 25, 1518: "Literature is flourishing, men's minds are awakening: it is a joy to live."

With the return of winter, Brant's health became progressively worse. In April, 1521, the city council, perhaps prompted by the Emperor, asked his opinion on how the imperial court could prevent the influx of the clergy into the monasteries. We do not have his answer. Other documents, however, in the political correspondence of the city or in the archives, dated between February and April of 1521, mention him or represent drafts by him. Apparently the last document on which he worked is dated April 20–21 —only nineteen days before his death. It contains a note by him on another document concerning a publication against Luther that Brant had proscribed. This proscription was now to be reconsidered. Thus it appears that he was active to within two or three weeks of his death—in this particular case concerning the most burning question of the day. His tombstone states that he died on May 10 of that year.

CHAPTER 3

Brant's Literary Work Prior to the Narrenschiff

I Literary Apprenticeship

PERHAPS soon after he had secured his baccalaureate in 1477 Brant began composing occasional verses, announcements, and letters—all now lost or unidentifiable—to accompany volumes published during the early years of printing in Basel. Such an early date for this activity is likely since Heynlin, who probably recommended him to the printers, spent most of his time in Basel between 1474 and 1478 and soon had come to know Brant well. The absence of specific references to Brant in the books of those days may mean merely that, being still an unknown tyro, he worked anonymously.

Among his oldest extant literary works are Latin exercises in distich form—broadsides—commenting on unusual happenings of the day. Several fairly early efforts of this kind, though in all likelihood not the earliest, are preserved in his *Varia Carmina:* two on floods of the Rhine in the Basel area in 1480; another, already mentioned in Chapter 1, on a solar eclipse of 1485 (in German as well as in Latin); and a fourth, in two Latin versions, on a hailstorm in 1487. They may be considered a crude form of early journalism.

Both poems of 1480 are Humanistic and pedantic products, typical of their time. The first, eighteen lines in length, asks Neptune what he is up to, warns him of dire consequences, and contains references to Deucalion, the dryads and fauns, Panis (deity of the staff of life), Ceres, Bromius (i.e., Bacchus, protector of the vineyard), and Pales (the ancient Italic god of the field). The second, a single distich, is a sort of chronogram (the letters of the words adding up to the date of composition, e.g., a = 1, b = 2, etc.). It is addressed to Pales, whose festival was observed April 21, the time of the flood.[1]

The fourth poem in two versions, like the third a chronogram, refers to a storm that occurred July 6, 1487. It records the loosening of tiles and bricks and the destruction of roofs. In the first version, the hail is personified and taken to task for its perfidy, as Neptune was in the poem mentioned above.[2] In general, the Latin of all these early efforts, like the German translation of the third, is faulty.

Early, too, is Brant's poem on his election as king of the carnival in 1482. He writes: "As king I live in hope, though fate may be invidious./ Though you, Fortune, have been able to make a poet king,/yet you cannot bring it about that such a one be king for long. . . . After you have taken away everything I will still remain/such a poet, poor as I am among the poor." [3]

Several mediocre early political poems, incorporated in the *Varia Carmina,* should also be added: two on Maximilian's election to the kingship, and the hyperbolic lines on his capture at Bruges. The following lines occur in the first poem on Maximilian's election: "Another of Caesarian seed has been sent from heaven./ You, Maximilian, are the bringer of peace to the world." And the second one states: "The Roman king shall not be opposed./ You, Maximilian, shall be the One adornment of the Empire." [4]

In the poem cursing the people of Bruges for making Maximilian prisoner, Brant fulminates: "Let no good faith be shown them, may they perish! Let that be the condition./ Let them suffer with penance the punishment they deserve./ It is proper and lawful for this city to endure the plow./ Let their accursed property be levelled to the ground. . . . Thus the ancient Germans deemed it honorable,/thus ancient virtue and power admonish the Empire." [5]

The first definite indication of Brant's collaboration with a printer is found in editions of two works of St. Augustine already referred to in Chapter 1: *The City of God* and *The Trinity.* They were published by Amerbach in 1489; each contains a poem by Brant. A third volume, consisting of *Sermons,* followed in 1494, and with a poem by Brant. In 1498 these poems were fused into a single undistinguished *carmen* of one hundred and six lines entitled "Ad divum Aurelium Augustum" and incorporated in the *Varia Carmina.* In 1493 Brant also helped Amerbach with a three-volume edition of the works of St. Ambrose, contributing a sixty-eight-line poem that is reproduced in a revised form in the *Varia Carmina*.

It is not known when the early hymn *Ave praeclara*, a translation from the Latin into the vernacular, first appeared.[6] However, we do know the publication date of four other translations, all of which were popular medieval works: *Thesmophagia* (1790); and *Cato, Facetus,* and *Moretus* (all in 1796).[7] As has been pointed out, internal evidence of a linguistic nature indicates a very early date for the hymn and also earlier dates of composition, namely, prior to 1490 for the last three. For that reason, these works deserve further discussion.

Ave praeclara is in the form of a sequence. Composed in sixteen strophes of varying length—from two to twelve lines—and with rhyme schemes that favor the feminine (*wercken-stercken; zieren-füren, geben–schweben–leben*), the poem's form is superior to its style and diction.[8] As a translation it is inferior to Brant's later rendering of *Ave, salve. Ave praeclara,* however, has a literary history. The oldest text, framed by an engraved border, is in St. Gall, but the better known and superior one, used by Zarncke in his edition of the *Narrenschiff*, was printed in Tübingen and is accompanied by music and by a woodcut depicting the Virgin over a cross. This Tübingen version, with some changes, appears in the *Gesangbüchlein* of Michael Vehe (Leipzig, 1537) under the title "Ein geistlich Prosa." In this form it is reproduced by Phillip Wackernagel in two editions of his *Deutsches Kirchenlied* (first edition, Stuttgart, 1841).

As to the four German translations on behavior—if their writing actually antedates the *Narrenschiff* (between the late 1480's and 1490)[9]—they indicate an inchoate interest in subject matter closely related to the *Narrenschiff* and have a style foreshadowing it. The didactic-satirical vein found in the latter can also be detected in these translations. *Cato,* a poem of six hundred and sixty-seven lines in the conventional free four-beat iambic couplets, preceded in the Furter edition of 1496[10] by eight Latin distichs, and followed by two more, suggests many topics found in the *Narrenschiff;* lines 376–99, for example, presage subjects dealt with in Chapters 6, 9, 41, and 97 of Brant's chief work. *Facetus,* some one hundred and fifty lines shorter than *Cato* and followed by eleven Latin distichs, is little more than a supplement of *Cato;* lines 3–4 state this: "As I am able, I add to Cato's teachings." [11] The purpose again is to teach manners, good breeding, and common sense (*gut sytten, zucht, vernunfft alltag*) by affirmative or negative precept. *Moretus* has the identical purpose and about the same length. It contains a Latin preface of eight distichs addressed to Brant's son Onuphrius, who was about ten when this work was published, and who is urged to benefit by its teachings. In one respect it differs from the two preceding works. It specifically details the qualities desirable in men of various professions and walks of life—clergy, layman, judge, physician, soldier. *Cato,* too, when published, was addressed to Onuphrius.

Brant's translations, so far as they could be compared with the Latin originals, seem as literal as may be reasonably expected. In the dedicatory Latin lines on *Moretus* to his son Onuphrius he emphasizes this: "I strove to render the Latin word for word" . . . (*scripta latina/ Ex verbo verbum reddere nisus*). As for content, therefore, little Brantian originality can be sought or found in them.

As in the case of *Ave praeclara,* the literary history of these translations is worthy of attention. Of *Cato,* as Brant wrote it, at least sixteen editions followed the original up to 1517, published in Basel (Bergmann, 1498; Lamparter, *ca.* 1506), Strasbourg, Nuremberg, and Augsburg, as well as elsewhere. *Facetus* was also issued at least sixteen times up to 1518 in various places, including Mainz and Leipzig, but *Moretus* four times up to 1508 —in Basel, Constance, and Strasbourg. Of *Thesmophagia* (1490, 748 lines)[12] there seems to have been no second printing; it appears to be the only one of these four poems published (without any indication of a printer) soon after it was written.

Brant's first, and only somewhat original, textbook, *Expositiones sive declarationes* . . . , a work done hurriedly on the basis of the lecture notes of one of his students, has been discussed in Chapter 1. Among the many later editions referred to there, it is of interest to find that the second, also under Furter's imprint (1500), is provided with some verses of Brant addressed *ad studiosos iuris.* Furter also published a third, fourth, and fifth edition (1503–1505). Besides, editions appeared in Angermünde (1514), Paris (1518), Lyons (1518), and a late one in Venice

(1584). The work won universal acclaim not easy to achieve in those days.

Brant's other early text, the *Decretum Gratiani* . . . , was provided with glosses by an Italian professor and with a woodcut representing Gratianus,[13] a poem by Brant, and the prose epilogue already referred to. This work, too, went through several printings, the most important of which was the 1500 edition of Amerbach and Froben. This contains—behind the index—the same woodcut, also three distichs by Brant, and the epilogue found in the first edition of 1493. The redaction, completed shortly before Brant left Basel, contains a dedication by him to the archbishop of Besançon, Francis of Luxemburg.

II *Preparation for Major Works*

A collection of Decretals in five books ordained by Pope Gregory IX before the middle of the thirteenth century, edited with parallel passages from Scripture and published by Froben in 1494 (second edition by Froben and Amberbach, 1500), contains a poem by Brant. We may assume that, in addition, he was largely responsible for the editing. He praises the work as being a credit to Basel. It is possible that it was Brant who suggested publication to Froben, as he often did in the case of works that were to his liking. As we saw, he was rarely known to lend his name to a project he did not wholeheartedly approve.

The brief verses or broadsides on disasters or natural phenomena like floods, eclipses, or hailstorms were followed in the 1490's by others with accompanying woodcuts. But some of these later ones are different in that they associate the natural phenomena with human events, usually with a warning that such an extraordinary happening is to be interpreted as a portent.[14] The idea can be traced to the ancient historians. Brant may have encountered it in Livy. Often, too, these broadsides occur in both Latin and German, like the one of 1485. That Brant addressed various types of readers on various levels, depending on interest and intellectual horizon, is shown also by the broadsides written in both languages. The Latin version differs from the German. Whereas in the former, for instance, the Church is stressed, it usually plays only a minor part in the latter.

One such broadside in two languages, printed by Bergmann,

and already mentioned is *Von dem Donnerstein gefallen . . . vor Ensisheim* (the Latin republished in two versions in the *Varia Carmina* as *De fulgetra immani . . .* and *Fulgetrae immanis . . . iaculatae in naeniam mortis optimi imperatoris Friderici consolationemque . . . Divi Maximiliani explanatio*). It tells of a meteor that fell in 1492 on a suburb of Basel. This is interpreted by Brant as a portent—indicated in the second title, warning of the death of Emperor Frederick III and foreboding evil for King Charles VIII of France, the foe of Maximilian.

The original woodcut shows, on the left, a town labeled Ensisheim, on the right another, Battenheim. A man on a horse and one on foot are fleeing in panic. Amid lightning a huge rock is falling from a cloud. The execution of the woodblock is crude. The German version, an acrostic, has been reproduced twice with textual variants, once in Berler's *Chronicle,* and again by Peter Merian.[15]

A broadside of a different nature, which does not deal with a freak of nature, although it again sheds glory on Maximilian, deals with the victory of the Germans over the French at Salins in 1493 (*Von der erlichen schlacht . . .*). Signed by the author, as is almost every work of Brant from about 1490 on, it informs us that its author wrote the one hundred and fifty-nine lines in a single hour.[16] Its quality makes this not incredible. Bergmann was its printer.

Different is the broadside *Vita sancti Onofrii* of 1494 (Bergmann), reproduced in the *Varia Carmina* (forty lines) and accompanied by a ten-line comparison of the labors of Onofrius and Hercules. Onofrius (or Onuphrius) was one of Brant's favorite saints whose hermit life he sometimes envied. Indeed, he named his eldest son for him and in the *Varia Carmina* also dedicated to him a three-hundred-line poem written in complicated Greek and Roman meters, which he pedantically identifies in every case, as was the Humanist custom. One strophe is described as "distrophon dicolon ex Heroico et dactylico Archilochio dimetro catalectico." The poem ends pleasantly with the eight-line "monocolon ex dactylico Adonio dimetro catalectico:" "Gentle Onofrius,/pray zealously for me/who sing of your/splendid deeds:/ Avoiding lowlier/places,/bring it about that I may become the equal of you/in my hour of death." [17] In the same poem

Brant pleads: "So I pray to you, blessed Onofrius,/remember your Sebastian." (*Ergo te precor, beate Onofri,/ Sis memor tui Sebastiani*).

Another broadside of a religious nature is a twenty-four-line German version of an old so-called *Verbum bonum* (i.e., *Ave*). It begins "Let us sing the word *Ave*" (*Das wort ave lond uns singen*). It is a product of the early 1490's and bears Brant's name in the title.[18] The cut represents the Virgin with the child in her arms, and two angels bearing a crown. There are also a prayer in prose and musical notations.

Brant also wrote other religious poetry before embarking upon a different course in his *Narrenschiff*. One of the most ambitious poems of this kind is his *Rosarium ex floribus vitae passionisque domini nostri Jesu Christi consertum* . . . ("Rosary woven of the flowers of the life and passion of our Lord Jesus Christ . . ."). After being published separately, probably in 1492, this Sapphic and adonic piece of fifty strophes (preceded by an introduction) was reprinted in the *Varia Carmina*. A feeble German version is also extant;[19] it probably appeared simultaneously with the Latin. In this poem, each strophe representing an *ave* of the rosary, the life of Christ is related from birth to death with what Schmidt (I, 266) calls "an austere nobility." But the flaws in Brant's pedestrian achievement remain.

Religious overtones are also present in the Froben edition of *Rhetorica Divina* (1492) of William, Bishop of Paris, for which Brant supplied verse proclaiming that prayers are, after all, far better than the orations of the ancients.

Reference has been made to Brant's first collection of poems, brought out by Bergmann in 1494. It is also religious in nature, "in praise of the Virgin Mary and many saints." Each of the eighteen poems of this now extremely rare work is headed by a woodcut, reminding one of the *Narrenschiff* in this respect. These poems are little more than exercises. Brant was undoubtedly a religious man, but he shows little real warmth toward his subject here. Artificiality and a concern for the technical features of his verse—and even these not always metrically correct—seem to have been paramount in his striving as a Humanist for technical finesse. His word order is forced and sometimes difficult to unravel, his conceits are far-fetched and pedantic, and although he does not attempt centos, the reminiscences of Classical authors are more numerous than original turns of phrase. However, since all these faults were not unusual among the Humanists, it would be unfair to blame him entirely for the common practices of his day, especially since these very practices were considered an essential part of good poetry by those learned contemporaries for whom he was writing.

For a book on the conquest of Granada, achieved in 1492 by Ferdinand the Catholic, the friend and sponsor of Columbus, Brant composed a congratulatory poem in fourteen distichs, "In Bethicum triumphum," published in 1494, in which he expresses the wish that Germany, too, might have a king like Ferdinand. "Then," he exclaims, "the whole world would soon be subject to our laws." [20] But perhaps with the feeling that the enthusiasm prompting these words may have carried him too far, he adds that Maximilian, too, would be only too happy to achieve such glory if he had more loyal followers. He fails to remind his readers, however, that Ferdinand not only had loyal followers but also a world power to back him up.

This book appeared in 1494 under Bergmann's imprint and seems to have been inspired by Brant. It is accompanied by a work of Carlo Verardus, as well as by a drama, and the famous Columbus letter to Raphael Sanchez, "De insulis nuper inventis," published twice by Bergmann. The publication of the letter in this work, with which we know Brant was involved, proves that he was familiar with the discoveries of Columbus. Indeed, he may well have induced Bergmann to publish the volume. Shortly thereafter he alluded to these discoveries in Chapter 66 of the *Narrenschiff*, saying it is better to lead a Christian life than to travel to parts unknown. [21]

Tritheim's *De scriptoribus ecclesiasticis*, published in 1494 by Bergmann and also mentioned in Chapter 1, contains articles on many men of Brant's acquaintance, among them Heynlin, Wimpheling, Geiler, as well as Brant himself. Concerning Brant, Tritheim writes that through his learning and literary activity he has added remarkable glory to the famous German city of Basel. [22] Tritheim's work, though published under his name, was actually a product of cooperative endeavor. Brant, for instance, contributed a glowing article on Reuchlin, whom he praises as learned in Hebrew, Greek, Latin, French, and German, as a writer of works of lasting quality on ecclesiastical and secular subjects, and as a translator of Greek Classical writers such as Homer, Xenophon, and Socrates into Latin as well as German.[23] Besides, Brant supplied nine conventional distichs for the colophon.

In the case of a few of the major and incidental writings preceding the *Narrenschiff* heretofore discussed, some bearing the date of 1494, composition and even publication may have occurred slightly later. But we assume that they were already in the hands of the printer when the *Narrenschiff* appeared at Shrovetide.

The period of Brant's literary life that has been discussed in this chapter, approximately the first fifteen years of his activity in this field, may be considered as the time of his apprenticeship and preparation for the two major works that were to follow— the *Narrenschiff* in 1494 and the Latin treatise on Jerusalem, *De Origine et conversatione bonorum Regum* . . . in 1495. It was a wide range of writing that engaged his attention. As many as a dozen different types or genres can be distinguished. They will be discussed in detail.

If, at first glance, these various literary undertakings seem heterogeneous, more careful examination shows that, as was suggested at the beginning of Chapter 2, they all fit into a pattern that dovetails with the scheme of the *Narrenschiff* and the Latin *De Origine et conversatione*. . . . The broadsides and their illustrations contain the same sort of informal comment on contemporary matters as does the *Narrenschiff*. The didacticism found in other types is of the same brand as that in both major works and serves an identical purpose. Not only would it inform; it would admonish readers of their obligations to the Church, the body politic, and society—primary purposes of Brant's literary activity. Finally, the religious motivation, inextricably interwoven with moral and political concerns in Brant's philosophy, is at the bottom of all his thought. It dominates both major works.

As was suggested in Chapter 2, these writings also served another important end. They show Brant as a pioneer in seeking new subject matter for literary treatment in an era when social changes demanded novel themes. The courtly literature produced by the small knightly class had in Brant's time lost its audience and appeal. A literature addressed to wider circles became necessary. This literature, whether in Latin or in German, would have to win adherents in much broader circles, among the clergy high and low, the scholars, and, most important, the emerging middle class.

Brant was anxious to reach all these and wrote on their various levels: here paratactic, brief, and serial; there in involved, complex clauses; here emphasizing one set of interests; there another.

As Brant developed it, this new literature was characterized by homely satire; moral preachment; didacticism; frequent recourse to the Classical tradition of Greek and Roman antiquity (to which many Humanists felt linked as by an unbroken chain), but set within a strictly Christian framework; contemporary appeal; and concern for the glory and welfare of Church and State, which could only be impeded by the folly of its people. Both Church and State together formed the concept of the "eternal" Holy Roman Empire.

If for Church and State we substitute religious denomination and political region, it may be said that much of the literature of Germany during the next one hundred years was built upon these foundations.

CHAPTER 4

History and Characterization of the Narrenschiff

I History

THE literature of fools and their follies begins long before Brant's time. In the Old Testament, the foolish are distinguished from the wise. Both Greek and Roman Classical literatures speak of fools. Northern European literature of the twelfth and thirteenth centuries brands the wayward and violent as fools (*toren*) and, using the Bible as a guide, contrasts them with the wise. A German adaptation of a moralizing Italian work of Tomaso Leoni by Hans Vintler, written in 1411 and entitled *Pluemen der Tugend* ("Flowers of Virtue," printed in Basel [1486]), contains illustrations of fools clad in flowing robes, each playing on a reed. Around the middle of the fifteenth century, *la sottie* was a popular type of literature in France, from where it spread to the Netherlands and Denmark. The early German Shrovetide plays of the fifteenth century, mostly anonymous, present many kinds of fools, as does the Swiss Felix Hemmerlin in his *Doctoratus in stultitia* ("Doctorate in folly"), edited by Brant, with other writings of Hemmerlin, in 1497. At least two anonymous collections of eight rhyming broadsides, with cuts illustrating fools, stemming probably from the 1480's[1] may, like Vintler's *Pluemen der Tugend,* be deemed forerunners of the *Narrenschiff.*

Brant found another obvious source in tales, by way of mouth, about the foolish carousers in the fabulous "land of milk and honey" known in the German of that time as *Schluraffenland,*[2] in France as *Coquaigne,* in the Netherlands as *Cockaenghen,* and in England as *Cockayne.*

France, we noted, indulged in her *sottie* in the fifteenth century, but England had been introduced to a Latin "Mirror of Fools" (*Speculum stultorum*) as early as the twelfth century by Nigel Wireker. In the fifteenth century, an English *Order of*

Fools by John Lydgate appeared. Chaucer was familiar with the former. Both Wireker and Lydgate were satirists, aiming their darts at the clergy. Wireker is the more sprightly. His hero is an ass that seeks a longer tail, visits foreign lands for the purpose of studying, and founds a new religious order which will permit him to do as he pleases. Lydgate's work, a catalogue of fools, is dull in comparison. He stresses their potential danger to society. Among their "follies," deceit and duplicity are stressed, while in Brant there is more emphasis on sensuality and riotousness of every kind. At least twenty of Brant's chapters deal with such "follies" or at least touch upon them. Herford judges that these were the chief national vices of the respective countries at that time.[3] But Brant knew of neither Wireker nor Lydgate.

The idea of the *Narrenschiff* as a series of brief chapters in verse, each depicting a different type of fool, may have come gradually to Brant and to the printer Bergmann, whose shop was new at that time,[4] and who wanted to make this work a success. It is possible that Brant first wrote separate chapters which served as handbills or broadsides, on the order of the anonymous ones mentioned above. These may have been the earliest publications of Bergmann after he had left Furter to establish his own shop. Since there were many wood carvers and other artists in Basel at the time, as well as printers who specialized in illustrated books, Bergmann had no trouble enlisting a corps of these. The idea of a volume of such chapters may then have followed as a matter of course. The artists probably worked in collaboration with Brant himself. With the possible exception of Chapter 48, "A Journeyman's Ship," the first sixty-two chapters, or approximately one-half of the work, were thus executed.

II *Characterization*

The scheme of the earlier chapters is fairly uniform. Each begins on the left-hand page with a three-line motto, followed by the woodblock, which takes up two-thirds of the page, and four lines of text. The opposite right-hand page contains thirty additional lines of text, so that the entire chapter usually consists of thirty-four lines. However, some of these early chapters— eleven of the first sixty-two—add two more full pages of text, permitting the next chapter to begin on the left-hand page. Except for chapter 48, which, with its full-page block, fits into the plan of the second half and the *Vorred,* or "Prologue," only Chapter 58, with one extra line, deviates from the scheme prevailing in the first half.

In the second half—Chapters 63 to 112—the woodcuts appear either on the left- or the right-hand page, and the chapters range in length from thirty-four to more than two hundred lines. Another more striking difference between the two halves is that in the first a *ship* of fools is referred to only occasionally and casually, while the ship is much more present in the second half and in the *Vorred,* which was written last.[5] It must be assumed that only the notion of a ship was in Brant's mind at first, but gradually gained more prominence. Yet in spite of the title of the book, the ship never became more than an incidental feature of Brant's work, a place where the fools could be herded together. At no point does the idea of a ship become the basis for a narrative plot. Brant never aimed at such a narrative.

The conceit of a ship on which roisterers are gathered either for a cross-country trip (on a *car naval,* or "carnival float") or a sea voyage is found before Brant's time in many places from the Netherlands to France and Austria. Of the greatest interest is a jocular academic oration delivered in Latin by Jodocus Gallus at a meeting in Heidelberg late in the 1480's. This address was given from a platform intended to simulate a ship, and the meeting was presided over by Brant's friend Wimpheling, who had the oration published in 1489 under the title *Monopolium et societas vulgo des Liechtschiffs* ("Monopoly and company of the light ship").[6] The accompanying woodcut shows a ship laden with passengers sailing through the air; it bears some similarities to one of the cuts prefacing the *Vorred.* The fact that Brant's friend Wimpheling presided over the meeting at which the address was delivered, and that it was published in Brant's native town, indicates that he was familiar with it.

Another possible source for Brant's idea of a fools ship is a sermon about a spiritual ship of fools, *Disz ist ein hubsche predig* . . . ("This is a charming sermon . . .") delivered a generation before the *Narrenschiff* on St. Ursula's day (October 21). It describes twenty-one dolts journeying on a fools ship pursued by Christ, who walks on the waves and urges them to desert their bark and board St. Ursula's ship, a vessel of penitence, which follows the Savior.[7] Besides anticipating Brant's concept, it seems to be a source for Geiler's *Schiff der Penitentz und Busswirkung* ("Ship of Penitence and Confession" [Latin, 1512; German, 1514]) and reminds one of the *St. Ursulae Schifflein* compiled by the Carthusian monks of Strasbourg in 1497 on the pattern of Brant's *Narrenschiff*. It also calls to mind Brant's Chapter 103, in which the fools ship is contrasted with St. Peter's vessel.

Brant's use of the ship, then, no matter how unimportant it may be in makeup of his work, did not stem from an original idea. Aside from the *Vorred,* where not only a ship but an entire fleet traveling on land and sea is mentioned, and Chapter 48, which introduces the journeyman's ship, only Chapters 103 and 108 deal importantly with the subject, the former dealing with the Antichrist, the latter with the *Schluraffen.* The latter takes up the subject of one of the cuts accompanying the *Vorred.* Both chapters stress the fate of any fools' fleet—destruction. Brant repeats this in the preface to the first edition of Locher's Latin version (1497): "Without ado we are destroyed; you see the endless number of fools/ that go along" (*Ilicet, obruimur: numerum sine fine videtis/ Qui comitatur*). In his sermons on the *Narrenschiff,* Geiler echoes this thought.

The purpose of the fools' voyage as Brant describes it has been variously explained. Perhaps Murner's suggestion is best, namely, to colonize the world with those fools who may survive the journey. Their starting point is Narbonne (Sorbonne?), their destination Narragonia, a fictitious country that suggests Aragon, with the German *Narr* prefixed.

Dancing is mentioned occasionally in the *Narrenschiff.* It is possible that the *danses macabres—Totentänze*—served Brant at certain points as a source. These dances were known through illustrations in editions published in various parts of Germany and accessible when Brant wrote, for instance in Mainz, Ulm, and Lübeck.[8] Fools' dances are referred to in Chapters 1, 61, 62, and 85, and some of the dance scenes depicted are reminiscent of woodcuts illustrating the *danses macabres.*

In a sense the *Narrenschiff,* however well constructed, is a compilation. At the end Brant himself says: "Here ends the *Narrenschiff,* which is compiled for usefulness . . ." (*"Hie endet*

sich das Narrenschiff, so zu nutz . . . gesamlet ist). But it is not
a compilation in the form of a patchwork made up of other
writings. Like the *bispel* of the time (a handbook aimed at moral
teaching), however, it offers a wealth of authorities to support
its preachment. No matter what the subject, most chapters, in
buttressing the argument, offer several references to the Bible
and to biblical characters, to the body of canon law, the Church
Fathers, and ancient history and literature, as a rule in that order.[9]

Brant favors the Old Testament, and especially the Book of
Proverbs and Ecclesiastes. Among ancient Greek and Roman
writers, Homer, Xenophon, and Plutarch, Ovid, Virgil (but only
spurious writings), Juvenal, and Seneca, and less often Catullus,
Cicero, and Horace, as well as Persius, are called upon for testimony. More recent literature is either totally unknown to Brant
(e.g., Chaucer) or, if known (e.g., Freidank), is not mentioned,
probably because such authors are not considered authoritative.
Some chapters are based almost exclusively upon a single authority, as Chapter 112 upon the pseudo-Virgilian *Vir bonus*. The
quotations are never haphazardly arranged. In marshalling them,
Brant shows a definite feeling for orderly design.

Brant's Humanist friends were enthusiastic about the *Narrenschiff*. In *De scriptoribus ecclesiasticis,* Tritheim called it a "divine satire" and deemed it the most sanative and amusing book
of his time. Nor was Tritheim the only contemporary to call the
work a satire. In a letter to Amerbach on August 1, 1497, Kraft
Hofmann inquires about an allusion of Brant "in his outstanding
satirical poem called The Ship of Narragonia" (*in praestantissimo
satyrico suo carmine Narragonie navis nomine*).[10] Wimpheling,
concerned with education, wanted it introduced into the schools.
Locher's circle praised it to the skies as the first book of a German
to wed the German language with poetry, and Locher himself
saw in Brant a Dante. Hutten said that Brant had written German
poetry according to a new principle or set of rules (*nova lege*).

How are we to explain such exuberant praise, since today the
Narrenschiff is not rated nearly so highly? Critics of our own
time agree in saying that it is a pedestrian patchwork of sins,
follies, faults, and foibles of its era presented without perspective.
They claim that its only saving graces are its humble, quotable
sententiousness, its skilful versification, its woodcuts, and its value

in documenting the intellectual and moral history of a mediocre epoch.

We must conclude that the *Narrenschiff* has been completely misunderstood in our time because we have lost the criteria by which alone its true qualities, so highly praised during Brant's own era, can be judged. In reality the work presented something entirely new for its time. One of these new features is that it was written in accordance with strict laws of form that tie it together into a connected, concordant whole.[11] The result is a harmony of content, desired effect, and expression. Here, perhaps for the first time in German literature, we can sense a writer's philosophy of life. This is a world view that discloses man as the central figure on earth, faced with the necessity of deciding whether he will take the path of wisdom and be a microcosmic image of the macrocosm, or will prefer to follow the path of folly and subvert that image.

Examination of the individual chapters shows that they faithfully follow the patterns demanded by ancient and medieval rhetoricians in developing their argument. Scrutiny of the pseudo-Ciceronian *Rhetorica ad Herennium* reveals that Brant makes scrupulous use of the devices of rhetoric described there, especially *expolitio* and *rationatio*.

Chapter 31, for instance, "Of Seeking Delay," illustrates *expolitio*, whereby a single idea is treated by demonstration and illustration from different points of view. The three-line motto connects the contents of the chapter with the cut and expresses an adage that contains Brant's judgment of the case. It ridicules those who put things off until tomorrow, and it states that the man who always sings "Cras, cras" (Latin for "tomorrow"), like a crow, will remain forever a fool.

The first ten lines comment on this and illustrate its truth. Brant says that when the Lord warns a fool to mend his ways and to give up his sinning, the fool asks for more time and croaks "Cras," not realizing that his time on earth is limited. The next five lines comment on the fact that while sins and folly attract eager crowds, righteous deeds are performed with sluggishness and delay. In lines 16–18 Brant, in reverting to the beginning of the chapter, lets the prodigal son postpone contrition until the morrow.

These four parts correspond in every detail to the four parts of what the *Rhetorica* calls the *expolitio*, which shows forth an idea from different angles, reverses the thought, which here turns from evildoing to righteousness, and then stresses the truthfulness of the lesson to be taught by stimulating the reader to join the author in thinking it through.

Then in ll. 19–20 there follows a simile, just as the *Rhetorica* prescribes: the "tomorrow" promised by the fool may never come but may melt like snow. Next comes a metaphor, again as demanded by the *Rhetorica*: only after the soul has gone will that tomorrow dawn (ll. 21-22). Now a *fictio personae* ("imaginary person") is described as heedless of his soul (ll. 23–24), and this is followed by the *exemplum* of those Jews who God decided must perish in the wilderness (ll. 25–28). The ending takes the form of a three-part *conclusio*, with repeated reference to what preceded: (1) Repent today, for tomorrow may add new sins; (2) God is calling you today; tomorrow He may be silent; (3) Many have been lost while waiting until the morrow to make amends. In these later sections, too, the chapter is patterned exactly upon the *Rhetorica*.

Ulrich Gaier calculates that almost 40 per cent of the chapters of the *Narrenschiff* employ *expolitio*. On the other hand, almost 50 per cent of the chapters are composed in the style that the *Rhetorica* calls *ratiocinatio*, a form of proof or means of convincing a listener by argument that starts with a general point of departure and reaches a definite conclusion. Chapters 71–73 fall into this category. Chapter 71: If you had rather go to court than eat, especially if you have a weak case, you should "apply nestles to your seat" (*das er am ars hett hächlen schwär*). Chapter 72: Insist upon being a coarse fool, or playing the boor and ruffian, "and you will gain mockery and rue" (*doch werden sie zu letst zu spott*). Chapter 73: Be sure you are qualified before deciding to become a priest; it would be better to close the religious orders than to have members who disgrace the frock.

Brant employs yet a third rhetorical form in presenting his fools. It is styled *narratio* in the *Rhetorica*. Occurring by itself in some chapters, but occasionally also in conjunction with *expolitio* or *ratiocinatio*, it is depiction pure and simple, as the Latin term implies, and is used to present the truth or to satirize the foolish world round about. Most of Chapter 75, "Of Bad Marksmen," is a case in point. It argues, not without tart humor, that hunting, jousting, and competitive shooting, when practiced to excess, as was often the case in Brant's day, are a waste of time.

These are rhetorical devices Brant employs in the individual chapters; but he also groups and balances his chapters according to a plan, at least in the first half of the work and in the first few chapters of the second half. Comparison and contrast are both used. According to a principle of unity, the chapters are inter-related, with cross-references serving his interest in theological, philosophical, and educational problems. Thus the Old Fool of Chapter 5 who teaches his son the pranks he himself can no longer play, is paralleled with the one in Chapter 6, who lets his children grow up to be Catilines; and the greed of the fools in Chapter 3 is matched by the greed and stinginess of those fathers in Chapter 6 who engage poor teachers for their offspring. The glutton who thinks only of food (Chapter 16) is as bad as the miser who loves his gold (Chapter 17) or the greedy hoarder (Chapter 3). The man who would serve both God and the world (Chapter 18) is contrasted with one who is insolent toward the deity (Chapter 14).

Chapters 17–30, when analyzed as to subject matter, appear to be a well-coordinated group, dealing in general with the desire for advancement at the expense of others. So, too, Chapters 40–42, which teach the reader to be deaf to folly but to learn from its mistakes, as well as from the wisdom of others. So, too, other chapters, but each group in a different way. Chapter 51 harks back to Chapter 39, both dealing with a secret betrayal. Whereas the man of true wisdom is referred to in the earlier chapter, the prophet is quoted in the latter.

And so, although each chapter is separate and deals with a special kind of fool, many point to other chapters or are set off against others through basic ideas. The untrusting patient and the good physician (Chapter 38) contrast with the trusting patient and the poor physician (Chapter 55).

With Chapter 67 a different procedure is introduced. While the earlier chapters are of a descriptive order, Chapters 67–98 are more argumentative and demonstrative. The first half of Chapter 75 is satirical, the second half allegorical. Chapter 99 on the decline of the faith and the plight of the Empire, is in the form of a refutation; Chapters 100–102 on flattery, gullibility, and falseness, offer a peroration. Chapters 100–112 are neatly tied together by means of three principal ideas of falseness, truth, and wisdom. Here Brant achieves a climax. These final chapters are what the Roman rhetoricians called the *suasoria,* or exhortation. This *suasoria* arouses initial fear of the Antichrist but subsequently hope that wisdom will save men.

Once having discovered that Brant has planned his work methodically, we can better appreciate the care with which he has constructed it.

Another characteristic of the *Narrenschiff,* often overlooked by modern critics, is its satire. It was for this that Brant was praised highly by some of his contemporaries. To be sure, a few recent writers have also emphasized the presence of satire in the *Narrenschiff,* especially Rainer Grünter[12] and Paul Böckmann.[13] But Gaier has pursued the matter further. Using the remarks of Tritheim, Locher, Wimpheling, and Hutten, he comes to the conclusion that Brant's work is consciously written in the tradition of the Roman *satura* of Lucilius, Horace, Persius, and Juvenal.

Not infrequently Brant quotes the Roman satirists, especially Juvenal, and although his ideas on the origins and historical development of the Roman *satura* were probably vague and uninformed, as were those of his contemporaries, he had read widely enough in the genre to understand it. He is not so much the wrathful judge of morals, like Juvenal, as he is the critic of human conduct (collecting books, overdressing, playing the boor, the prattler, the glutton), like Persius, endowed with a strong ironic vein. This, too, lends Brant's work a unity of purpose, a single-mindedness characteristic of the Humanist striving for closed, rounded-out form. And he chose the vernacular because he wanted to reach the common classes and strove for informal conversational verse in the style of the Horatian *sermones,* or conversations. Hand in hand with this went a desire to help the cause of the Holy Roman Empire by making its people worthier of its mission.

The *Narrenschiff,* then, is not an unsuccessful epic, as it is usually styled by its condescending critics today, but a well-planned, successful revival of the Roman *satura,* with all its richness and many-sided appeal, and with hints of a Renaissance world-view.

Modern writers have also charged Brant with lumping all the sins, follies, and foibles of his compatriots together as folly, or *Narrheit*, without perspective, gradation, or a sense of comparative importance. Such charges are ill-founded.

These follies may be classed under six general headings: (1) vicious or criminal offenses; (2) insolence; (3) riotousness; (4) sloth; (5) presumptuousness; and (6) mere perversities, foibles, or peccadillos. Under the vicious offenses would fall the "folly" of adultery (Chapter 33), licentiousness (Chapter 50), and blasphemy (Chapters 86–87). Chapters dealing with insolence are: Chapter 14, "Of Insolence toward God"; Chapter 42, "Of Scorners" (especially those who scorn the counsel of the wise); and Chapter 43, "Contempt of Eternal Joy" (those who indulge in the pleasures of the world). Riotousness is illustrated by Chapter 16, which deals with gluttony and feasting; and sloth is accorded a whole chapter (Chapter 97) because it leads to wickedness. Presumptuousness is evidenced by contempt of Holy Writ (Chapter 11), by the carping critic who does no better than those he criticizes (Chapter 21), or by the prideful fool who forgets humility (Chapter 92).

These manifestations of what Brant calls "folly" are all serious and worthy of censure or satire. However, they reveal marked differences of degree. Certainly adultery and blasphemy have been deemed graver in any age than sloth, riotous living, or pride. But if this is so, what are we to say about those "follies" that may be classified as mere perversities—among them collecting books merely as a status symbol (Chapter 1), or slavishness to styles of dress (Chapter 4), or roistering (Chapter 27), or creating a disturbance during church service (Chapter 44), or dancing (Chapter 61), or working on holidays (Chapter 95)?

A satire may attack anything from a sin to a peccadillo, so long as the author considers his subject important enough for satirical treatment. But Brant, though mentioning penalties, does not mete out to his fools any condign punishment suited to the gravity of the folly. He consigns them all to Narragonia, and indeed in Chapter 103 (on the Antichrist) and Chapter 108 (on the carousing *Schluraffen*) threatens them with shipwreck. Moreover, in his preface to the first edition of Locher's Latin version, he fore-tells destruction for *all* his fools, regardless of their folly.

Why, then, are all follies alike to him? To find the answer, we must turn to those four contemporaries of Brant who influenced him profoundly: Peter von Andlau, his professor of canon law in Basel; Johann Hugonis, whose famulus he became; Johannes Heynlin von Stein, his brilliant confidant and mentor; and Geiler, the preacher and orator.

The ideas he derived from them, already discussed, need only be summed up here: the divine mission of the German people to hold the Roman *imperium* and to rule the world; the laxity of manners and morals among the Germans as a threat to this hegemony, on the principle of *noblesse oblige;* the need to eradicate not only the cardinal sins but even their peccadillos, all of which contribute to their decline; the necessity of awakening their conscience by preaching to them in the vernacular in a satirical, folk-oriented vein.

These were the ideas that shaped Brant's concept of folly, and they explain why he held that even slight eccentricities stand in the way of German greatness and world leadership, and will lead to ruin. And ruin to Brant is a two-headed menace. It may come in the form of *Weltende, Weltuntergang,* or as the triumph of the heathen Turk, a fear he eloquently voices in Chapter 99 of the *Narrenschiff.*

But most clearly did Brant express these convictions in that lengthy and revealing poem, "De corrupto ordine vivendi pereuntibus," which he wrote as a preface to the third edition of Locher's Latin version of the *Narrenschiff.* The snatches already quoted from it are pertinent here, too. Similarly appropriate passages are: ll. 9ff.: "We see all the fools plying their oars without rule or order and not setting their sails properly./ Thus they are driven by the vortex to Scylla, the Syrtes, the shoals, and Charybdis,/ to suffer shipwreck." Again, ll. 13ff.: "I find that all fools have perished in this way:/they transgressed, they transgressed their bounds and left the path/that God and the proper orderliness of things dictate./ All things that live in the heavens, on earth, or in the water,/are served by orderliness." [14]

In this spirit Brant satirizes even the seemingly slightest flaws of his countrymen as follies leading to destruction, for they run counter to and obstruct the divine mission of the German people. They violate the *ordo vivendi,* orderly living, the fitness of things, the quotidian things—what Von Andlau terms *ordinatio dei.* Those guilty of such violation must perish. Even a false show of learning or foppishness thus becomes a sign of decadence, which cannot be tolerated in an age when the "God-chosen leaders" of Christian civilization—the German people—are struggling for survival. Only wisdom sent from heaven can save them.

As Henry Charles Lea remarks in his article, "The Eve of the Reformation," in the *Cambridge Modern History,* Brant's work is "a singularly instructive document for the intellectual and moral history of the period."

III *The Woodcuts*

Brant's teachings in a spirit of humorous, though also testy, moralistic didacticism, his down-to-earth aphoristic style, and his careful craftsmanship, as well as the fact that he pillories all the faults of the average person of the time, so that each can find something of himself, went far to make the work popular. But no less important were the excellent woodcuts in the early editions and translations in an age when reading was a rare accomplishment. In these woodcuts, each fool is depicted in a typical way, alone or in a group, the blocks measuring 3 1/2 by 4 1/2 inches, and in several cases 4 by 6 1/2 inches. A few of the cuts recur in later chapters, and a few chapters lack a cut. Six variant cuts were introduced in the second edition of 1495. With some changes and additions most of the cuts were used or revised for over a generation and copied even in the foreign translations. They reappeared in 1520 in the German edition of Geiler's sermons on subjects in the *Narrenschiff.* The later editions omitted them, although some of the later translations contained copies of them, and, in a few cases new cuts. But they were not republished in their entirety until Simrock reproduced them in his modernized German translation (1872). Authentic reproductions are found in the facsimiles of the first edition of 1494 by F. Schultz and H. Koegler, both of 1913, also in Zeydel's English translation, and, most recently, in Manfred Lemmer's little volume.[15]

In the nineteenth century some critics, among them Charles Schmidt, believed that Brant himself was responsible for these cuts, but there is no evidence whatever for this. It does seem likely, however, that Brant himself offered suggestions and ideas for their execution. Nor are they all the work of a single artist. At least four wood carvers contributed work, and it is now generally recognized that the master artist was Albrecht Dürer.[16]

Taking hints from his own teacher Michael Wolgemut, as well as from the copper engraver Martin Schongauer, Dürer here developed an entirely new style. Up to this time, the wood carvers had practiced a technique of contours, only suggesting the rest of the picture. Now for the first time Dürer revealed an inchoate realistic technique, noticeable also in the forty-five cuts he made for the *Ritter vom Turn* at about the same time. Although his innovations are not uniformly successful, on the whole they are bold, agile, and clever. Each of his fools is individually conceived, each has his own characteristic expression. Later artists seem to have been influenced by the style of the *Narrenschiff* cuts, for example Hans Weiditz, who in 1532 illustrated Petrarch.[17]

The background against which Dürer presents his fools is also individualized and differentiated. Here we find a landscape, there a farmyard, here a bird, there an animal. Even the garments of the persons depicted are distinguished by their cut or their folds. Such realism as is found in these backgrounds had never before been essayed in woodcuts.

Among the criteria Winkler used to determine that Dürer himself created over 70 per cent of the cuts were their fine quality, their artistic and stylistic similarity to other works of his dating from the same period, the fact that he was in Basel for a comparatively long time during the very period when the *Narrenschiff* must have been created,[18] and a peculiar signature: a row of little bells on the fools cap running in a line from the middle of the forehead up and then back to the nape of the neck halfway between the ears.

Almost eighty of the woodcuts have thus been assigned to Dürer, among them that of the front title page, Chapter 6 on "The Teaching of Children" (also Chapters 7 and 8), Chapter 13 on "Amours" (also Chapters 14–16), Chapter 20 "On Finding Treasures," Chapter 22 "On the Teaching of Wisdom," Chapter 27 "On Useless Studying," Chapter 29 "On Judging Others" (also

Chapters 31–32), Chapters 34–48, and so on. Lemmer's book, pp. 135ff., identifies them all.

When work was started on the *Narrenschiff*, two artists were probably set to work, Dürer and the nameless wood carver now known as *Haintz-Nar-Meister* ("Hank-Fool-Master"), so named from the superscription over the woodcut to Chapter 5 on old fools, which he created. He was probably the leading Basel wood carver of his day, though not of Dürer's stature. In only two— perhaps his earliest cuts (to Chapters 1 and 5)—he imitates Dürer's signature of the row of little bells. Certain other characteristics of his work distinguish him from the master. His fools are larger in stature; his execution is monotonous; he lacks wit and imagination and employs little realism; his figures usually want animation. In his background he often replaces realistic detail with mere hatching. But sometimes he achieves pleasing, decorative effects and good composition, thanks to a keen power of observation.

When Dürer left Basel in the latter part of 1493, the work of illustration was not yet finished, although he was active on the later chapters, making fifteen cuts for the last nineteen chapters. The "Haintz-Nar-Meister" had contributed twenty-one cuts, among them those to Chapters 1–2, 4–5, 12, 17–19, 21, and 23–24. Probably two additional artists were then engaged, one now called *Gnad-Her-Meister* ("Mercy-Lord-Master") in accordance with the superscription on his first cut (to Chapter 3). His figures are lively and expressive, but the faces of his fools are coarse or even grotesque. He fails in perspective, and in composition achieves only chaos. He was also responsible for the cuts to Chapters 11, 25, 28, 49, 66, and 83. The fourth artist supplied only three inferior cuts, done hastily in the general style of the "Haintz-Nar-Meister," and impressing one as unfinished. They are the cuts to Chapters 97, 98, and the all-important Chapter 99.

The problem faced by all the artists alike was not easy to solve. They were called upon to depict the gist of a text often difficult to capture in a single picture. Although, as we have seen, Brant's chapters have a remarkable basic unity and cohesion, they could be approached by the illustrator from various aspects. The result is that different methods of representation were used. In some of the cuts, the general contents of the chapter is well caught (e.g. Chapters 1 and 6); in others a proverb or single thought is capriciously singled out (Chapters 2 and 8); in some the motto alone is considered (Chapters 7 and 9). Very often Brant's picturesque language has helped the artist to deal with such abstract concepts as licentiousness, marriages of convenience, blasphemy, or adultery. Since the relationship between motto and illustration is often closer than that between illustration and text, we may perhaps assume that Brant sometimes wrote the motto to suit the picture.

Frequently, however, marked differences are to be noted between the cut and the text. While the text often contains more than the cut, the opposite is at times true. The cut to Chapter 103 (by Dürer) is a case in point. It reminds one of the medieval allegories. In the foreground we discover the apostle Peter with his attribute, the key. He is pulling St. Peter's skiff (the Church) ashore. In it are righteous passengers. The cut does not, however, suggest the danger to which Brant says the skiff is exposed. But on the keel of a wrecked ship of fools the cut does reveal the Antichrist, into whose ear Satan is blowing evil. In his right hand the Antichrist is holding a bag of money, to be used for bribery, and in his left a scourge, a sign of his power. Several shipwrecked fools are drowning with their false books. Other skiffs are bearing fools toward the Antichrist. We are reminded of some of the Reformation caricatures.

In general it may be said that the *Narrenschiff* woodcuts deserve more study than has been accorded to them. The allegorical element in particular requires closer scrutiny. The work itself, however, is not allegorical. The better cuts—and every student of the work soon singles out his favorites—can be studied and admired a long time, and still new allurements will be found. They show deftness and distinct virtuosity but at the same time simplicity and naturalness.

Brief comment on Brant's language and verse in his masterpiece will perhaps be appropriate in closing this chapter. The text of the work is uniquely authentic because Brant himself saw it through the press and allowed only a few misprints to escape him. The German dialect is the one prevalent at the time in the region from Basel to Strasbourg, perhaps a bit standardized to resemble a literary language that did not yet exist. It is the Alsatian dialect (Alemannic), and Early New High German, not Middle High German. The orthography is still uncertain, especially in the case of the consonants. The rhyme is fairly pure within the framework of Brant's own speech, which, however, was hardly stabilized and not well enunciated. His prosody is very good for the time, and his verses are more regular than those of his contemporaries. This must have been in Hutten's mind when he praised Brant for having "forced the vernacular into smooth verse" (*barbaraque in numeros compellit verba ligatos*). The meter is technically known as iambic dimeter, that is, two pairs of iambic feet to the line, with each pair of lines rhyming.[19]

CHAPTER 5

The Narrenschiff *Calls at Many Ports*

I *Editions and Reprints*

FEW secular books can boast of so rich a literary history and so profound an influence, not only in their own country, but also in half a dozen foreign lands, as the *Narrenschiff*. Let us consider first the editions and reprints.

During the twenty-seven years remaining to Brant after the initial appearance of the work, six authorized editions were published. Several excellent copies of the first exist, one in Berlin[1] and another in Dresden being the most complete. On twenty-four pages of the various copies, some of which have been preserved in incomplete or fragmentary form, textual variations may be noted, indicating that Brant made changes during the printing. No doubt he also did the proofreading, yet at least twenty-five misprints remained.

The second edition, of 1495, also printed by Bergmann in Basel, contains the two new chapters mentioned before, which were inserted after Chapter 110 as Chapters 110a and 110b. The third (Basel, Bergmann, 1499) adds a "Protestation" of forty lines (usually known as Chapter 113), attacking the unauthorized reprints and adaptations, which had already begun to appear, especially the plagiarized Strasbourg interpolation of 1494. The fourth edition, which appeared in Basel in 1506, continues to bear the name of Bergmann as the printer, as does the fifth (1509). The sixth and last (1512) came out not in Basel but in Strasbourg, and was printed by Matthys Hupfuff.

But besides these six authorized editions, not less than seven unauthorized ones appeared in southern Germany. Three, with changes in dialect only, appeared in 1494 in Reutlingen, Nuremberg, and Augsburg. Four others, two by the Strasbourg printer Grüninger of 1494 and 1497, and two by an Augsburg printer of

1495 and 1498, contain arbitrary alterations, for most of which Grüninger was probably responsible.

All the subsequent editions and reprints were issued after Brant's death, appearing in the sixteenth and seventeenth centuries without the woodcuts. At least seven editions were issued between 1553 and 1625 in Frankfurt and were sold in the fairs held in that city. As late as 1574 a reprint came out in Basel. Most of these redactions are characterized by arbitrary changes in language and content, and are addressed to Protestant readers. The majority are shamelessly plagiarized from original editions. Some contain additional works by other authors.

Within a period of one hundred and twenty-five years, twenty-nine more or less faithful editions and reprints appeared. But the Reformation slowed the book's progress considerably. The Thirty Years' War put an end to its popularity. and no new edition appeared until Strobel's redaction of 1839.[2] It has been used to advantage by almost all succeeding editors, especially Zarncke,[3] whose edition of 1854, now available in a reprint (1961), was long considered standard and indeed is still indispensable even after the appearance of Schultz's and Koegler's facsimiles of 1913 and Lemmer's edition of 1962.

Lemmer's redaction is primarily a text edition, prepared chiefly on the basis of the Dresden copy of the first edition, but also with attention to the second and third editions of 1495 and 1499, respectively. The introduction is brief, but a valuable and up-to-date bibliography is added to it. Where Zarncke includes only four of the woodcuts, Lemmer, in his first edition, gives five but has supplemented these with reproductions of all the blocks in the Insel Verlag publication discussed in detail in the previous chapter.

II *Translations and Adaptations*

In spite of the eclipse suffered by the *Narrenschiff* for some two hundred years—from approximately the 1630's to the 1830's—over forty editions and reprints have appeared from 1494 to the present time. Counting the translations and adaptations that began appearing from 1497 on in Latin, Low German, French, Dutch-Flemish, English (both sixteenth-century and modern[4]), modern German, and more recently, Russian,[5] we find that in some form the *Narrenschiff* has appeared on an average of one edition every six years, and that more than half a dozen countries have been involved over a period of four hundred and seventy years.

The earliest, it seems, and most significant translation, suggested by Brant himself, was the Latin rendering of Locher (or Philomusus Suevus). In less than five months its first edition was exhausted. During its first one hundred and seventy-five years it went through at least nine editions. Brant contributed importantly to it, writing various prefatory poems not only for the first edition but also for the third of 1498. Locher changed the arrangement of the chapters and, in his first edition, omitted Chapters 36 and 74-75.[6] He placed Chapter 46, "On the Power of Fools," after Chapter 64, "On bad Women," and added new material to Chapters 48, 108, and 111. Instead of Brant's three-line motto heading each chapter, Locher composed two elegiac distichs. The body of the chapters is in dactylic hexameters or elegiac distichs, while Chapter 111 is composed in Sapphic strophes.

However, the difference between Brant's original and the Latin version of Locher goes deeper. Brant stresses the fiction of a ship only in the second half of the work; Locher does so throughout —a fact which influenced almost all the other translators. The tone of Locher's work is more formal and more learned, with many Classical allusions. The book reproduces only a fraction of the ideas and a still smaller part of the wit and popular sententiousness of the original. Although offering all the woodcuts, with but a few changes, it is much less faithful in other respects and may be termed a very free adaptation. Often, too, it abbreviates the chapters, Chapter 66, for example, being cut from one hundred and fifty-four to thirty-four lines. All this was probably done with Brant's approval. The book's transcending importance lies in the fact that, written in the international language of the day, it rather than Brant's German work, became the basis for virtually all the other translations of the fifteenth and sixteenth centuries, except the Low German version. Thanks to Locher, the *Narrenschiff* became the first work of German origin to enter the mainstream of European letters. More than that, it was even instrumental in turning that stream in a new direction.

It is possible that the Low German (or more exactly, Low Saxon) rendering, *Dat narren schyp,* which was widely read in northern Germany, is even older than Locher's Latin adaptation. The first edition appeared in Lübeck in 1497 and is believed to be by Hans van Ghetelen. The second revised edition came out in Rostock in 1519.[7] The translation of Van Ghetelen is based primarily upon two of the early unauthorized editions—the Nuremberg redaction of 1494 and, to a lesser extent, the Strasbourg redaction, which had come out in the same year.

In important respects, this Low German version is more faithful to Brant's original than is Locher's Latin version. It retains the homely tone, the humble sententiousness which appealed to the masses, as well as the satire, wit, and irony. It also adheres to the sequence of chapters established by Brant. Through it the *Narrenschiff* achieved more than regional triumph; it became a German classic which could be understood by people in every part of the German-speaking area. Another characteristic of this version is that it clearly reveals an effort to propagandize Brant's ideas by means of new original material of a polemic and moralizing nature. Most critics today believe that the same Van Ghetelen who translated the *Narrenschiff* into Low German was also responsible for *Reynke de Vos,* the beast epic (Lübeck, 1498). If this is true, he has the distinction of being associated with the two German works of the fifteenth century that can claim international distinction.

In France, the *Narrenschiff* also enjoyed wide dissemination in the vernacular for about a hundred years. Three separate paraphrases—hardly translations—appeared between 1497 and 1499. The earliest of these, prepared anonymously by Pierre Rivière in Paris,[8] is based upon the first edition of Locher. Rivière deserves praise for making a valiant effort to adhere faithfully to the only source he seems to have known, but despite his conscientious endeavor he bowed to the inevitable and turned out an adaptation of what itself was only a free verse adaptation. The result, accordingly, is a work far removed from Brant's original. Around 1535 an abbreviation of Rivière's adaptation appeared.

In 1498 the second French version, by Jehan Drouyn, came out in Lyons. It is a considerably abbreviated reworking, mostly in prose, of Rivière's effort in verse. Some indications point to the possibility that Drouyn also used one of the later editions of Locher's Latin translation. Parts of the Drouyn version consist of passages in verse drawn directly from Rivière, without any changes. Drouyn's work, too, seems to have achieved considerable popularity, for a reprint was published in 1499, and a third edition as late as 1579.

Finally, a third French version, in prose, prepared by an anonymous writer, appeared in Paris in 1499. It was published by Marnef and is usually referred to by that name. There is no evidence that it is based either on Rivière or Drouyn; it seems to be an independent adaptation taken from one of the editions of Locher. It continued to be bought for about two generations. A new edition appeared in Paris in 1529, and another in Lyons in 1530. Thus, aside from editions of Locher's Latin *Narrenschiff* published in France, that country was provided with at least eight French editions, which supplied the demands of French readers from 1497 to about the end of the sixteenth century.

A Dutch-Flemish version of the *Narrenschiff* was published at Paris in 1500 by G. Marchand (or Coopman). It is recorded by Van Praet in his *Catalogue des livres imprimés sur velin de la bibliothèque du rois*[9] and also referred to by Aurelius Pompen in *The English Versions of the Ship of Fools*.[10] Primarily it is based upon Locher but secondarily also on the French Rivière. It forms the basis for five later Dutch editions[11] dated 1504, 1548, 1584, 1610, and 1635, respectively. The 1584 edition, a copy of which is in the Cornell University Library, was edited by Jan van Ghelen. These numerous editions show without a doubt that the *Narrenschiff* achieved great popularity in the Lowlands and retained that popularity for almost one hundred and fifty years.

It is surprising that a second Latin version of the *Narrenschiff*, *Navis Stultifera*, appeared as early as 1505—only eight years after Locher's first edition and its reprintings. It was prepared by the Paris bookdealer Iodocus Badius Ascensius and published by Marnef and Badius. Its basis is the 1498 Paris edition of Locher. Being an adaptation of what had already proved to be an adaptation of the original—quite like Rivière's French version—it is very far removed from Brant, and a feeble effort. Some chapters are mercilessly cut, among them Chapters 48 and 108. In spite of its grave defects, it proved popular, as a Basel reprint of 1506 and at least four later redactions[12] indicate. But aside from the title and the woodcuts, this pirated product of Badius has little in common with Brant's *Narrenschiff*.[13]

Late in 1508 or early the next year, Alexander Barclay, an English priest who seems to have been of Scottish provenience, published the first English adaptation in uninspired Chaucerian stanzas and called his work *The Shyp of folys of the worlde . . . translated . . . out of Laten, Frenche, and Doche into Englysse tonge.* It was published by the famous English printer Richard Pynson. Two subsequent editions appeared during the late years of the sixteenth century—in 1570, published by Cawood, and in 1590.

The basis for Barclay's work is definitely one of the two 1497 editions of Locher, but there is transposition of chapters and much new material.[14] He also used Badius and Rivière. He copied Brant's woodcuts, recut by Pynson to the size of the originals. On the title page as well as in his introduction Barclay mentions having used Brant, but this is definitely false. In fact, he refers to Locher's Latin as though it were the original.

As has just been suggested, Barclay also knew Rivière's French adaptation. Indeed, he made important use of it, as internal evidence indicates, and in all likelihood became acquainted with the *Narrenschiff* through Rivière. This need not surprise us if we recall that the early sixteenth century in England saw the gradual spreading of the French Renaissance influence.[15] It seems a curious quirk of literary history that a work which is in itself secondarily related to the Renaissance as is the *Narrenschiff* should enter England on the wave of that movement.

Barclay's language is a compromise between the literary English of his time and the vernacular of the middle class. Much of his text, especially as regards allusions and references, is new and takes the place of passages in Locher which he probably deemed less appropriate. At the end of the chapters he often adds what he calls *Envoys,* or concluding stanzas, which serve as moralizing summaries of the subject matter treated in the chapters. In general his text is longer than Locher's, a seven-line strophe sometimes taking the place of from two to four lines of Locher's. When he depends upon Rivière, as he frequently does, he is likely to copy his errors. On the whole, Barclay does not reproduce Brant's, nor even Locher's, ship of fools. His is a new ship which carries the fools of sixteenth-century England.

The following sampling of Barclay's style is from Chapter 62:

> He is a foole that wandreth by night
> In fielde or towne, in company or alone,
> Playing at his lemmans doore withouten light,
> Till all his body be colde as leade or stone:
> These fooles knocking till they feele no colde,
> Shall it repent and feele when they be olde.
>
> Now would I of my boke have made an ende,
> And with my shyp drawen to some haven or port,
> Stricken my sayle, and all my fooles sende
> Unto the lande, a while them selfe to sporte.
> But this my purpose is letted by a sorte
> Of frantike fooles, wandering about by night,
> For often all evill doers hateth the day light.

A two-volume reprint of Barclay's work appeared in 1874,[16] with an introduction by T. H. Jamieson. Various literary anthologies reprint selections from it.

Of less merit than Barclay's version, and yet of great importance, is the competitive prose redaction of Henry Watson entitled *The Shyppe of Fooles* and published by Wynkyn de Worde in London in 1509. A second edition appeared in 1517. Watson's work is a literal translation of the second edition of Drouyn's French prose version. Only the mottos are done in verse.

Two years prior to the appearance of the Barclay reprint in 1874, Karl Simrock issued his modern German version of Brant's *Narrenschiff*, with all the woodcuts of the original edition. The recent English translation, with a full introduction, as well as the woodcuts, and in the meter of the original, by Edwin H. Zeydel, has been reprinted twice. Two new German translations, one selective, the other complete, also deserve mention, the first by Franz Hirtler, the other by Margot Richter, both with woodcuts. A Russian rendering appeared in Moscow in 1965.

III *Influences*

Although the subject has been under investigation for well over one hundred and twenty-five years, the pervasive influence of Brant's *Narrenschiff* on the literature and thought of Germany and at least four other countries, England, the United States, France and the Lowlands, not to mention Italy, has not been comprehensively studied. Surprisingly, the impact of this famous work in France and England stands out more sharply than does its influence in Germany, perhaps because its role in those countries was more limited and circumscribed.

In the German-speaking regions it seems to have been the Carthusian monks of Alsace who first manifested interest in the *Narrenschiff* when they published a book of excerpts which they called *St. Ursulae Schifflein* (Strasbourg, 1497). It has been referred to in the previous chapter. The Carthusians, with whom Brant had close relations, as we have seen, found in Brant's work a mine of maxims to guide Christians through life. Already at that time the *Narrenschiff* enjoyed fame as a lay bible.

Of greater influence were the one hundred and forty-two sermons in the vernacular, which were preached by Brant's friend Geiler in Strasbourg on subjects from the *Narrenschiff*. Geiler used his friend's original text, the Strasbourg redaction with interpolations, and the Locher translation. He employed frequent quotations but treated the text quite freely and added much original material. Not long after Geiler's death in 1510 the sermons came out in Strasbourg in Latin, with the original woodcuts and under the title *Navicula seu speculum fatuorum* ("Little ship, or mirror of fools"), edited by Jacob Otther. The work proved popular even in Latin, and other editions followed, among them a much-abbreviated German redaction, published in Strasbourg in 1520 by Grüninger and edited by Johann Pauli. This is notable as the last edition containing the woodcuts to appear before Brant's death.

The high but fully deserved praise which Brant's friends showered upon the *Narrenschiff* has been discussed. Prominent reference was also made to it in the famous *Epistolae obscurorum virorum* (Part II, epistle 9). But persons who were not necessarily close to Brant, or who were of the next generation and did not even know him, also paid homage to the *Narrenschiff* by imitating it—the sincerest form of flattery. Among them were Murner, Gengenbach, Hans Sachs, and Fischart, and, in the seventeenth century, Abraham a Santa Clara. Sometimes they were so completely under his spell that, for a while at least, they became his satellites; others used his ideas incidentally but strikingly enough.

Thomas Murner, the raucous Franciscan monk and student of Locher, who played a prominent part in Brant's later life in Strasbourg and who was seventeen years younger, felt his influence very strongly. His early works, for instance, the *Narrenbeschwörung* ("Fools exorcised") and to a lesser extent the *Schelmenzunft* ("Guild of fools"), both of 1512, were inspired by Brant and make much use of the *Narrenschiff*. Murner borrows passage after passage from Brant, as well as the woodcuts. However, he carries his satire further and uses different means of combating folly as a form of polemics.[17] Murner, though a learned man like Brant, made no display of his scholarship. He strove to be a man of the people, the crude, uncouth vulgarian. In his sermons, his method, though on a somewhat lower plane, is that of Geiler, whose style was discussed in Chapter 2. In his later works, for example, *Gäuchmatt,* the appearance of which was vetoed in Strasbourg, Murner leans upon Brant, as he does in *Von dem grossen Lutherischen Narren* ("Of the great Lutheran Fool" [1522]), but he goes his own way in his sharp attack upon Luther, whose advocate he had once been.

The German polemical literature of the Reformation period would be the poorer if it had not had Brant's gallery of fools to fall back upon. With the *Narrenschiff*, the *Narr* became a recognized type and a commonplace in German literature, being subjected to many forms of bizarre torture: exorcized, poured like lead, cut to a pattern, immersed, and devoured. German literature of the sixteenth century is rich in its use of such procedures.

Pamphilius Gengenbach is little known today but was famous in his time as a writer and printer. He spent about twenty-five years in Basel beginning in the second decade of the sixteenth century. He trained himself on Brant's style and language and turned out successful poems and dramas. Especially in his earlier writings, one can detect traces of Brant's influence—in expressions and entire lines, as well as in the choice of themes. He expanded Brant's Chapter 63 on beggars and made his *Liber Vagatorum* ("Book of Vagabonds") out of it.

Hans Sachs, the famous shoemaker and poet, a generation younger than Brant; and Johann Fischart, Sachs's junior by several generations, who next to Luther are probably the best-known German writers of the sixteenth century, were also under Brant's spell. Sachs is fond of taking examples from Brant, quoting passages from him at length, and expatiating upon them. Being naturally partial to humble aphorisms and clever sayings, he indulges this interest by putting many of Brant's saws to his own use. Fischart, the author of a kaleidoscopic satire in the manner of Rabelais, mentions Brant frequently and considers him one of his authorities and teachers. Both Sachs and Fischart delighted in fusing the grotesque middle-class humor of the fifteenth-century Shrovetide plays with Brant's stern, awe-inspiring manner as a wise teacher-preacher.

With these writers of the sixteenth century, the list of those who owed much to Brant is far from exhausted. There are numerous others. Some borrowed lengthy passages from him; others inserted Brantian quotations into their own works; and many more made Brantian fools and types the focus of their interest. It is regrettable, however, that in some respects the sixteenth-century authors learned nothing from him. They failed to profit by his prosody, his clear style, and his craftsmanship. Had they heeded this master and Luther also, they could have vastly improved their writing.

Much later, during the latter part of the seventeenth century, the popular preacher Abraham a Santa Clara (Ulrich Megerle) from Baden, who was active in Vienna, constructed his sermons on the pattern of *Narrenschiff* chapters and, as Murner had done, on Geiler's sermons—with homely puns, comical comparisons, and down-to-earth witticisms. By adjusting his mode of presentation to models as old as Brant and Geiler and castigating fools quite as they had, Abraham paid them a fine tribute.

In discussing the genesis of the *Narrenschiff* in the previous chapter, we saw that the idea of a *ship* did not play a decisive role in Brant's planning. In the present chapter, however, we noted that the idea became an important factor in most of the translations and adaptations. Posterity seems to have sensed its secondary nature, for it died out in Germany after Brant's death. However, the concept of the *Narr* as a type continued to thrive. Not only was he exorcized, as we saw above, he was also metamorphosed into various forms, becoming a dove, a bee, a hare, a worm, and even a Protestant devil.

As recently as 1840, a *Neues Narrenschiff* appeared in Germany, written by Felix Weickert.[18] It borrows only the title from Brant and is a collection of anecdotes and witty sayings. Appropriate illustrations were provided by Willibald Cornelius. The work was probably occasioned by the publication of Strobel's first nineteenth-century edition of Brant's *Narrenschiff* in 1839.

In the text and in footnote 13 (above), the appearance in Paris of a Latin imitation of the *Narrenschiff* by Iodocus Badius Ascensius (1501) was noted. Although restricted to the foolish antics of women, it is probably the earliest outright imitation of the *Narrenschiff* in any language. Soon after, Symphorien Champier, the physician of Duke Antoine of Lorraine, published a work of his friend Robert de Balsac (also spelled Balsat and Barsat), a royal counselor, chamberlain, and seneschal, and a famous warrior. It bears the title *La Nef des princes et des battailes de noblesse* ("The Ship of princes and battles of nobility"). It came out in Lyons in 1502. Bound with it was another pamphlet of Balsac, *Le droit chemin de l'hopital et les gens qui le trouvent par leurs oeuvres et manière de vivre* ("The right road to the poorhouse and the people who find it by their deeds and manner of living"). At least four new editions appeared over a period of one hundred and thirty-five years.

The *Nef* has only peripheral interest for this study because, prompted by the Drouyn translation (also published in Lyons), it pictures its princes as being aboard a ship—but not of fools! *Le droit chemin*,[19] however, is of immediate concern because, as in Brant, various types of people are depicted who because of their foolish ways go *a l'hopital* ("to the poorhouse"). Among them are those "who have little and spend much," or "who like to gamble but lose often," or those who with small incomes indulge in luxuries. Many of these improvident people—Balsac does not spare us a long list of them—are types familiar from Brant; others again are new. Also among those catalogued are merchants who extend too much credit; men bent on vengeance; servants who lose what their masters have entrusted to them, or who cheat their masters; people who are guided by the counsel of fools; those who vulgarly display affluence; gourmands; those who permit their domestics to carouse at night and sleep by day; those who sing *gaudeamus* ("let us have fun"), but never *requiem* ("rest"); and those who put off duties until tomorrow.

Besides the five editions of Balsac's little treatise appearing between 1502 and 1635, two very free imitations were published. All these are of paramount interest in the ramified history of Brant's influence in Europe. It colored the satire in Gringoire's *Les Abus du monde* ("The abuses of the world") and indirectly influenced also Desmoulin's *Le Catholicon des mal-advisez* ("Panacea for the ill-advised"), as well as two versified warnings by D'Adonville against sins leading to beggary.

The influence of Balsac's *Le droit chemin* was not restricted to France, however. In England Robert Copland's *Hye Way to the Spyttel House,* written about 1535, to be discussed below, and in the Netherlands an anonymous Dutch version of Balsac's pamphlet, prepared in the middle of the sixteenth century and published in Antwerp, appeared. The latter is called *Den rechten weg nae t' Gaesthuys* ("The right way to the guest house")—a title which like Copland's is quite reminiscent of Balsac.[20] Parts of this Dutch work are directly copied from Balsac; other parts are changed or expanded. Like all the imitators of Balsac, the Dutch writer introduces many innovations but unfortunately dulls Balsac's terse, pointed satire with a torrent of words.

A British scholar, W. G. Moore,[21] has suggested, plausibly enough, that possibly Rabelais, as a printer's reader in Lyons, became acquainted with the literary tradition of Balsac and his followers and was thus moved to the conception of *Gargantua* (1532).

Another striking indication of Brant's influence in France is found in a work published about 1503 by P. le Dru for A. Vérard in Paris. It bears the title *Les Regnars traversant les perilleuses voyes de folles fiances du monde, composée par Sebastian Brand* ("Rulers on the dangerous paths of foolish promises [. . .] by Sebastian Brand"). This outspoken satire on the manners of its time, which attacks all classes of society, was actually written by Jean Bouchet, historian and poet of Poitiers, as an acrostic in the

"Exhortacion" reveals. Its use of Brant's name on the title page is proof enough of his great popularity in France during the early years of the sixteenth century. Four editions of *Les Regnars* came out between 1503 and 1505, and two others in 1510 and 1522.

The last French work to be considered here is one by Balsac's friend Champier entitled *La Nef des dames vertueuses* ("The ship of virtuous women" [1503]). Like Balsac's *Nef*, it also uses the notion of a ship, though not of fools. The text itself is of no interest to readers of Brant, but a singular woodcut showing a ship at sea carrying the Holy Virgin, the child Jesus, Ste Catherine, Ste Barbara, and two gowned doctors reminds one of some of the blocks found in *Narrenschiff* literature.

Literature on Brant and the *Narrenschiff* in Italy is rare. As late as 1551, however, writings of Brant are mentioned in a Latin work of Lilo Giraldi on "Two Dialogues on Poets of Our Day," the title of which is *Dialogi duo de poetis nostrorum temporum* and which was published in Florence.[22] On page 65 we read concerning Brant: "There was also Sebastian Ticio, a German from Strasbourg, who wrote an infinite number of poems in his country, some of which were brought to Italy, as the 'Rosary of the Virgin Mary' in sapphics, and the 'Ship,' which is called fool-bearing." No further literature on Brant has come to light in Italy.

In the previous chapter Wireker and Lydgate were mentioned as predecessors of Brant in England. As for the influence of Brant's *Narrenschiff* in that country, it is stronger even and more pervasive than its impact in France, and constitutes one of the most striking examples of the infiltration of a Continental literary work into the woof and texture of English literature. It owes its impetus to Locher's Latin version, Barclay's and Watson's translations, and the various French imitations of Brant mentioned above. Nor was its life there limited to a short period; it lasted well into the seventeenth century. The lengthy list of English writings bearing the imprint of Brant's *Narrenschiff* begins with *Cock Lorell's Bote* and satirical verses of Skelton, goes on to Copland, and from him to Tarlton, Rowlands, and Dekker. Indeed, it was a commonplace in sixteenth-century England to refer to Brant's *Ship*. Sir Thomas More, for example, mentions it in one of his epigrams.

Although Brant's work encountered much stronger competition

in England, it held its ground there more steadfastly than in Germany itself. It did so, however, not as a German work, but rather as a book of uncertain foreign provenience which had become famous through English and French adaptations. As in France its effect in England was salutary, for it offered fresh stimulus and novel form to native satire, helped put an end to allegory, moralities, and personified abstractions. Thus it contributed to the development of satirical portraiture on the basis of social types. This opened the way to such genres as the drama, the essay, and the novel of character.[23]

The anonymous poem *Cock Lorell's Bote* (about 1510), which is preserved as a fragment, offers a picture of vagabond life in a lighter vein than Brant's *Narrenschiff*. Its chief ideas come from the English adaptations of Brant's Prologue, from his Chapter 48 ("A Journeyman's Ship"), but especially from Chapter 108 ("The *Schluraffen* Ship"), with the cut accompanying it in Watson's book. As in Wireker and Lydgate, a religious order of dolts is envisaged. However, the *Bote* can be called neither an adaptation nor an imitation of Brant. It is thoroughly English. Imagination, realism, vigorous treatment, and a sustained plot are its characteristics. The passengers on the *Bote* are jolly Londoners bent upon mercantile ventures as they travel through England in their fool's ship. Four of the Watson woodblocks serve as illustrations.

Skelton's *Boke of three Fooles* turns by way of Barclay to three other chapters of Brant, namely Chapter 50 ("Of Sensual Pleasure"), Chapter 52 ("Marrying for the sake of Goods"), and Chapter 53 ("Of Envy and Hatred"). The same writer's *The Bowge of Court* (about 1520), depending mainly upon Langland, deals allegorically with the follies and perils of life at court, but, familiar with Barclay, introduces Brant's idea of a ship and makes use of his Chapter 100 on courtiers. A third work of Skelton, *Colyn Cloute*, shows the impact of Brant's Chapter 73 ("Of Becoming a Priest").

Copland's *Hye Way to the Spyttel House*, mentioned above in connection with Balsac's *Le droit chemin*, deals with beggars. A short visit to the "Spyttel House" leads Copland to describe the inmates, who are bent upon self-destruction because of their own folly. As in the *Bote* and in the *Bowge*, the satire is directed at a single class. (cf. Brant's Chapter 63), but with more realism than in Brant and with some attention to plot. The transition from Brant to Balsac seems to have come about in three steps—through Locher, Rivière, and Drouyn. The transition from Balsac to Copland (probably by way of d'Adonville) is a classical example of French Renaissance influence in England.[24]

The Fraternity of Vagabonds by Awdelay has as its subject the Orders of Knaves which arose in England during the early years of the sixteenth century. The same writer's *Quartern of Serving Men* is traceable through the *Bote* back to Brant via Rivière, Barclay, and Watson. Copland's ballad *The Twenty-Five Orders of Fools* is surprisingly close to Brant in the types of fools treated.

Emblem literature, making its way to England a few generations after the appearance of Barclay's *Shyp of folys*, is well represented there by Van der Noot's *Theatre for Voluptuous Worldlings* (1569). Hardly had it appeared when a new edition of Barclay's *Shyp,* accompanied by Locher's Latin version, was published (1570).

The actor and clown Tarlton, a favorite of Queen Elizabeth who died in 1588, wrote a book, *A Horseload of Fools,* which is also indirectly under Brant's influence. It depicts a company of fools passing through Fleet Street in a pony cart, on the way to being exhibited in a puppet show. They represent various callings. A similar work is Armin's *Nest of Ninnies* (1608), the "ninnies" being court jesters who symbolize human weaknesses in general. Both works are satires of manners, replacing the satires of morals of a former day.

By devious courses, numerous other English works dating from the seventeenth century and later can be traced to Brant, among them Dekker's *Gul's Hornbooke* (1609), Rowland's *A Foole's Bolt is sone Shot,* and *Sixteen Knaves Marching in Order.* The dramatists had also heard of Brant, as references to him in Nashe's *Summer's Last Will and Testament* and Greene's *Friar Bacon* indicate. Robert Burton's seventeenth-century *Anatomy of Melancholy* also pays tribute to him. The term "ship of fools" remained popular as well. As late as 1807, an imitation in verse of Barclay's work appeared in London under the title *Stultifera navis, the Modern Ship of Fools.* And in our own day Katherine Anne Porter made the "Ship" popular again with her novel *The Ship of Fools* (1962)—

also on film—the plot of which, however, has no connection with Brant.

No doubt the most famous work on folly is the *Moriae Encomium* (1509) of Erasmus, embellished with the woodcuts furnished by Holbein in 1514. Erasmus undoubtedly became acquainted with the *Narrenschiff* before 1509,[25] for its imitator and translator Badius was a friend of his. Erasmus himself met Brant in Strasbourg in 1514, and probably again in Antwerp in 1520, and expressed great admiration for him.

There are many threads connecting the masterpieces of these two famous writers, although their relationship has not been studied exhaustively.[26] Erasmus represents a more advanced stage of Humanism and is more outspoken in his criticism of ecclesiastical abuses. Yet he follows Brant in many of his subjects, e.g., on amours, the parade of learning, drunkenness, self-love, flattery, sloth, sensuality, women as slaves of fashion, carousing, husbands' suspicion of wives, quack doctors, endless lawsuits, and many more. Verbal echoes of Brant also occur. Some of Holbein's woodcuts (e.g., Nos. 107 and 131) are reminiscent of *Narrenschiff* cuts.

However, Erasmus never copied or imitated Brant. Whereas Erasmus was more flippant, Brant was more religious, whereas Erasmus' style is more brilliant, Brant follows the best traditions of ancient rhetoric and satire. Whereas Erasmus is sparkling and subtle, Brant is more steadfast in purpose and idealism.

Gruenter, in his *Neophilologus* article, detects an unbridgeable gap between Brant and Erasmus. The former, he claims, could never have brought himself to write a book *in praise* of folly. But perhaps the gap is not as wide as Gruenter thinks. It should be remembered that Erasmus' work is a prosopopeia, in which not Erasmus but an imaginary person is speaking. Erasmus is playing a role. Similarly Brant lets the foolish old man (Chapter 5) or the *Schluraffen* (Chapter 108) speak. This suggests similarity of method and point of view. Moreover, both writers tie satire to paradoxical, demonstrative language. Accordingly, their differences are basically differences of personality.[27]

CHAPTER 6

Brant's Literary Work after the Narrenschiff

I *Later Works Written in Basel*

THERE can be no doubt that Brant was one of the more prolific and, in a limited sense, one of the most versatile writers of his age. Aside from his early works, which have been discussed in the last three chapters, he wrote some two dozen original treatises in numerous fields and edited, prefaced, or added other material to many more. In part these have already been briefly alluded to; they will be discussed in more detail here. However, no attempt at completeness will be made. Although it is true that Brant never set his name to any book the contents of which he did not approve, some of his writings or editions are of such minor importance or of limited, dated appeal that consideration of them would not be warranted in a work of the present scope.

Only to a restricted degree, and in keeping with a narrow type of classification, Hellmut Rosenfeld's division of Brant's works into (a) juridical, (b) religious, (c) political-historical, and (d) moral is a comprehensive and valid one.[1] Criteria of a descriptive nature, not only considerations of content, are required. Apart from satire, which is certainly a category of its own, this division gives no inkling of the important hortatory type of writing which was characteristic of Brant. It is found in the various exhortations, particularly those addressed to Maximilian, whether they be in the form of broadsides on significant natural phenomena,[2] or of learned and more sustained treatises urging an aggressive policy on the part of the Empire to defeat the Turks and recapture the Holy Land.

The most important writing of this kind is a book in Latin prose. It appeared about a year after the *Narrenschiff* (in 1495) and is entitled *De origine et conversatione bonorum Regum et laude Civitate Hierosolymae; cum exhortatione eiusdem recuperandae.*

Unlike the *Narrenschiff* it is of course not addressed to the common people but to the upper classes, particularly to the ruler himself and the princes. It may be described as Brant's most seriously meant, though not his most successful, work. Purporting to be a historical study, it is heavy with scholarship and its argument is supported by numerous authorities. In terms of ancient rhetoric it takes the form of a *suasoria,* like the final chapters of the *Narrenschiff.* In general it is constructed in accordance with the rhetorical rules Brant observed in that earlier work. It also reveals well-rounded form. Brant's purpose is to perform a task which he is convinced God has entrusted to him.

After a preface that is addressed to Emperor Maximilian, Brant recounts the origins of Jerusalem, the changes in its name, and the history of Jerusalem, of Palestine, and of the Jews at some length. There is also an account of the various attempts to restore the Holy Temple. Brant's sources are the Old Testament, including the apocrypha, the historians Josephus, Orosius, Martinus Polonus, Platina, and Sambellicus, as well as his own contemporary Aeneas Sylvius. Prosperity under good kings like David, and misfortune under bad kings like Solomon and Rehoboam, are deemed the doing of God himself. The destruction of Jerusalem is limned in elaborate detail, as are the life and crucifixion of Christ. The history of Antioch, too, is recounted.

The story of the founding and growth of Rome, as well as an account of the rise of Western and Eastern Europe takes up less space. Then the villain of the long narrative is introduced: The Islam, which is destined to play a major role. For the present the defeat of the Saracens by Charles Martel is gleefully related. In the ninth century we witness the Roman Empire passing on to Charlemagne, who, as Brant would like to believe, was the one who wrested Jerusalem from the Moors. With Charlemagne, regarded not as a Frank but as a German, the beneficent world rulership of the Germans begins. The period of the Crusades is then accorded some attention as a part of the military history of that age. Those emperors who were stirred by the crusading spirit are praised; Frederick II, however, is rebuked for his reluctance to participate in a crusade.

With the fall of Constantinople in 1453, Brant's survey reaches a sinister climax. Upon it he bases his main argument, centering on the necessity for Europe to unite under the imperial aegis against the common Turkish enemy. The Turk is bent upon destroying the Holy Empire of the German Nation, which is the heart of the Christian world. Various popes, says Brant, have tried to inspire the temporal rulers to action. But crusades and other joint actions by defenders of the faith have failed because the princes selfishly refused to join in a common endeavor. With Emperor Maximilian, however, a new era has dawned. Perhaps he will succeed where earlier rulers have failed. So at least Brant hopes.

Thus far goes Brant's historical account, which is based, in good part, on wishful thinking. In his final exordium, written more hastily, he once more finds the cause for the loss of Jerusalem to lie in the apathy of his Christian brethren and exhorts them to awaken and renounce their pride and vicious jealousy of one another. Here much is made of what he had already hinted at in his earlier account of the history of the Jews—the role played by good and bad rulers in the lives of nations. The bad ones, he avers, are not sent by God to punish the people, but to test their virtue, their mettle.

The work ends with a résumé and a plea in elegiac distichs, exhorting Maximilian to make war against the infidel and reminding him that wicked kings are only for wicked subjects. His final lines are: "Therefore proceed quickly, holy king, God on high has wished that you/be the harsh bolt of lightning against the Turks./ He will make the kingdom stable by blessing your scepter/as you hold the world under your heel. Farewell." [3]

Sinfulness, we are told, harvests only retribution. Consider the Greeks, Brant warns. They already suffer under the oppression of the Turk because they have renounced the Holy Father in Rome!

Reading this heavy-handed treatise in ponderous Latin, one is often reminded of much more succinct, effective lines in the *Narrenschiff*, Chapter 99, such as:

> So strong the Turks have grown to be,
> They hold the ocean not alone,
> The Danube too is now their own.
> They make their inroads when they will [4]
>
> . . . .
>
> For Europe's gates are open wide,
> The foe encircles every side,

With sleep or rest he's not content,
On Christian blood alone he's bent[5]

. . . .

Each prince would take a slice of goose
And pry himself a feather loose.
No wonder it's a platitude
That now our realm is bare and nude.[6]

. . . .

For things seem bad, whate'er I scan,
While living I'll warn many a man.
The frivolous who pay no heed
I'll give a fool's cap, that's their meed.[7]

It is worthy of note that in this lengthy Latin work Brant's treatment of Jews is remarkably objective for a Christian writer of the fifteenth century. His venom is not directed against them but rather against the Moslems.

Learned Humanist contemporaries were impressed with the book, and many expressed their satisfaction. When Hermannsgrün went to the Holy Land in 1504, he wished Brant could accompany him as an expert guide. Printed, as the colophon states, to honor the ruler—*in honorem sacrosanctae regiae maiestatis*—and containing a picture of Maximilian bearing a banner with a cross and receiving a sword and a palm frond from heaven, as a frontispiece, the work could leave no doubt about its hortatory and even importunate message. We cannot be sure, however, that the Emperor actually read it. As late as 1518 it was translated into German in Strasbourg by Casper Frey, a Swiss.

One other important work from Brant's pen, also published by Bergmann and, as we have seen, provided by him with a letter of dedication to Wymmar von Erkelenz, was published in Basel before Brant left that town—his collection of poems called *Varia Carmina*. Much, but by no means all of it, is of a religious nature, written in honor of the Virgin Mary and of various saints. In part it was taken over from Brant's earlier collection of verse, which it augmented.

Brant treats Mary as a loving mother, or again as an interceding friend; he also describes her grief over the passion of Christ. He reminds his readers of her feats and cites many prefigurations of her from the Old Testament, with which he shows a thorough familiarity. We have seen that he was a firm believer in the doctrine of the immaculate conception and, indeed, defended that doctrine in the *Carmina* and elsewhere. In one of his finest religious poems he prays that his own generation may be inspired to the full by the divine son to whom the Holy Virgin gave birth: "And may my day witness the God/to whom the Holy Virgin gave birth and who was once promised to the people." [8]

Another important feature of the *Varia Carmina* is Brant's preoccupation with the saints. He devotes poems to no less than forty of them, prominent among these being Onuphrius, the hermit, in whose honor he named his eldest son. But besides hermits he sings of saints noted for their great learning, of those who devoted their lives to helping the sick and the poor, and of those whom he could call upon in times of distress or special need. Sebastian, a military martyr, from whom Brant derived his own name, is also singled out, not in the usual distichs, but in forty Sapphic stanzas. Brant calls himself "an inexperienced lad" (*puer imperitus*), a formula of humility he affects in his religious lyrics.

Of another type are the numerous poems dedicated to illustrious friends, among them Heynlin and Geiler, Dalburg, bishop of Worms, Tritheim, Bergmann, Reuchlin, and Locher. Most of these poems appeared originally in volumes Brant helped to edit. Also noteworthy are the ten distichs on Petrarch that came out for the first time in a volume of annotations of his Latin works published by Amerbach in 1496. Brant declares that Petrarch's fame is so firmly established that nothing could be added to it and nothing detracted.[9]

Brant is aware of Petrarch's accomplishments as a Humanist and even seems to hint at his greatness as a representative of the Renaissance when he says: "He applied his mind to everything he could put to human/use, enriched with knowledge and genius." [10] Moreover, he refers to Petrarch's wide interests as revealed in his literary activities, but makes no special reference to his poetry: "Singlehanded he wrote many volumes on subjects/that had not been properly treated before." [11] In addition he praises him for "renouncing the world." [12]

Brant dedicated five distichs to the tenth-century nun Hrotsvit in recognition of the fame she had brought to Germany through her poems, plays, and historical writings, discovered a few years before by Celtes. Geographical places and establishments, even pastimes also serve as vehicles for his poems, as for instance the hot baths in Baden or the game of chess.[13]

Humor, an aspect of Brant's writing well documented in the *Narrenschiff*, is supplied by a prose piece inserted near the end of the *Carmina* and dedicated to the learned Saxon statesman, scholar, and orator Heinrich von Büno, who had just paid him a visit. It offers two jocular explanations why the clocks in Basel in those days were set an hour ahead of those in other cities.

Brant's mythological explanation is as follows. Before his expedition to fetch the cattle of Geryon, Hercules was commanded to travel twenty miles each day by daylight. Upon his return, he crossed the Vosges into Alsace, where even before that time Dionysus had planted vines. In Colmar he drank too freely of the excellent wines (called here *Rangeticum* and *Riceuillarium*, now known as the Rangen brand of Thann and the Riquewihr), fell asleep, and lost an hour in his schedule. When he finally awoke, he left so hastily that he forgot his cudgel (still a part of the Colmar coat of arms) and arrived in Basel after nightfall. To make up the hour he had lost, he persuaded the Baselers to set their clocks one hour ahead. Thus he could start with a clean slate on the next morning.

The alternative explanation offered by Brant is jocosely pseudo-historical in nature. Basilius, a Roman senator, he reports, was dispatched in the year 9 A.D. by Augustus together with Quintilius Varus to subdue the peoples east of the Rhine. After the defeat and rout of the Roman legions, Basilius thought the whole Roman Empire had been destroyed and Augustus dethroned. Eager to rescue at least his own name from oblivion, he resettled the colonists of the town of Augst (Augusta Raurica) and moved them to the present site of Basel, giving the infant city his own name. And in his haste to build the new town, he set the clocks ahead in order to gain an hour of daylight. "Basilienses vero in perpetuam horarum gloriam et mutati horologii commemorationem talem horae anticipationem et quasi divinitus eis auspiciatam hactenus observarunt," Brant declares.

Bearing in mind Brant's satirical bent, we may wonder if this *explanatio*, as he calls it, is not a sly dig at the people of Basel for their tendency to go their own way in stubborn defiance of others.

For in May, 1498, when this was written, marked hostility toward the Empire could already be noted in Basel, as well as a restless desire to break the imperial ties in favor of the Swiss Confederation—much to Brant's chagrin. The Baselers always want to be different from others, he avers, and when they are abroad delight in asking the time of day, only to boast: "But we are an hour ahead of you." [14]

In Chapters 2 and 4 another important work of Brant was mentioned. It is a poem of almost six hundred lines which served as a preface to an edition of Locher's Latin *Narrenschiff* and bears the title "De corrupto ordine vivendi pereuntibus." It was also incorporated in the *Varia Carmina*. In our previous references to it, the purpose was to emphasize its important bearing upon the *Narrenschiff*. Here, however, it must be considered as a whole and as an incisive revelation of Brant's philosophy of history, again markedly under the influence of Peter von Andlau, Hugonis, and Heynlin. It reflects the doctrine underlying the canon law of that era.

The permanence and success of bodies politic, argues Brant, depend on order. Insubordination is invariably followed by destruction. After the fall of the angels, God sent man to Paradise and gave him free rein. The demon, however, seduced him and caused him to be driven from the Garden of Eden. Then God saw fit to assume control again and to mete out just punishment upon man through the flood and the confusion of tongues. A survey of history shows that Assyrians, Persians, Medes, Jews, and Greeks all fell short of God's expectations—*ordine neglecto*—because they failed to observe the divinely decreed orderliness which alone befits man and leads him to prosperity and happiness. Rome, too, was lacking in this respect. Thereupon the Lord made Christ ruler, and Christ, in turn, entrusted mankind to Peter and his successors.

From that time on, two lights shone forth throughout the civilized world, the Pope and the Emperor: "These are the two great lights God created/to illuminate and irradiate the world." [15] The major light is the Pope, the minor the Emperor. And the "order of things" dictates that the lesser shall always be subordinate to the greater: "majori inferior subsit ubique suo" (l. 266; Zarncke, p. 124)—altogether in accord with Von Andlau's dictum in his *Libellus de caesarea monarchia*. But alas, sighs Brant, Daniel's dream and prophecy of the four beasts may yet be fulfilled. The

Germans have wielded the world scepter for seven hundred years. There is danger that it may be wrested from them. Beware of the year 1503, which may mark this event! Only if order is established —the Diet of Worms points hopefully in this direction—the poor are treated justly, the Emperor is assisted by his lords, the Turks are repulsed, and genuine peace is restored, only then will there be hope. Order, in public life and in the life of every subject great or small is the keynote. For "there is terror and constant wrong-doing whenever order is lacking" ("horror adest, errorque frequens ubi deficit ordo" [l. 523; Zarncke, 127]).

The ideological relationship between this important poem, the *Narrenschiff,* and the ambitious prose essay *De origine et conversatione* . . . requires no further comment. Nor should one, in this connection, overlook Brant's edition of Ludwig Bebenburg's *Germanorum veterum principum zelus* . . . , in which the princes are reminded that their predecessors observed orderliness and defended the Christian faith more actively and aggressively. Related to this in some measure is an edition of the Decrees (here styled "Panormia") of Ivo of Chartres, printed by Furter in 1499. Brant uses the dedication of the book to the Basel priest Johann Götz as an opportunity to praise the beneficence of law, order, and peace, and to lament their absence in Germany. This may well, he warns, lead to the end of the Christian world.

It is no coincidence that the same year (1498) which brought forth the philosophical-historical poem "De corrupto ordine . . ." saw the publication of the *Revelations* of the martyr Methodius, printed by Furter *opera et vigilantia Sebastiani Brant,* that is, with his editorial cooperation. For it was Methodius in *De consummatione saeculi* ("On the end of our age"), who had seen the vision of the last of the Holy Roman Emperors at his death depositing his crown on a cross in Jerusalem, and the crown returning to heaven while the end of the world ensued.

In 1498 there appeared another long poem—one hundred and eighty lines; its very title bespeaks its message: *Thurcorum terror et potentia* ("The terror and power of the Turks"). It represents the remarks of a Turkish grandee who fears no one but Maximilian and hopes to be converted to Christianity. This poem first appeared separately and was incorporated in a later printing of the *Varia Carmina.*

Jollier is Brant's German *Fuchshatz* ("Fox hunt" [1497]), which reminds one of the *Narrenschiff*. But here the fox, as the miscreant and deceiver, plays the role of the *Narr*. Here, too, we find appropriate woodcuts to accompany the text. Amusing also is Brant's Latin edition of the fables of Aesop, with additions of his own. It did not appear until 1501 in Basel in Pforzheim's shop but must have been finished before he left there. It is in two parts and, as a personal touch, contains a letter to Brant's son Onuphrius. A German edition of 1508 reproduces some of Brant's work.

Bordering more on the spirit of the *Narrenschiff* than his Aesop is Brant's work on the congenial satire of Felix Hemmerlin.[16] Brant edited Hemmerlin's *Opuscula et Tractatus* ("Little Works and Tracts") for the publisher Kessler in Basel in 1497.

An ambitious edition of the entire Vulgate Bible, undertaken jointly by Petri and Froben in 1498, also enjoyed the advantage of Brant's editorial help and was graced by his dedication of the undertaking to his friend Johann von Dalburg.

Apart from his teaching and law practice, Brant, during these latter years in Basel was much overworked by his activity for the publishers. Brief assignments, such as his distichs on Reuchlin's drama *Scenica progymnasmata,* or *Henno,* published by Bergmann in 1498, and his more copious lines to the same friend two years earlier,[17] were followed by an edition of the three books of *De Patientia* by Baptiste of Mantua (published by Bergmann in 1499). Brant also edited in 1499 the collection of the "Decrees of the Nominalist Basel Church Council," with which he, as a Realist, did not agree fully, though approving its stand against heresy, and for the immaculate conception.

II *Literary Activity in Strasbourg*

We turn now from Brant's activities in Basel to those of the last twenty years he spent in his native Strasbourg. Contrary to general opinion, his preoccupation with editing and publishing, we know, did not abate to any appreciable degree during this latter period. Noteworthy, too, is the fact that from 1501 on he wrote and edited more works of importance in German than in Latin.

The Latin edition of *The Consolation of Philosophy* by Boethius, with an epigram by Brant, was published by Grüninger in Strasbourg in 1501. Brant must have lost no time helping Grüninger. He took his oath of office in Strasbourg in January; the book appeared in September. Much more ambitious is the two-part volume of German "Lives of the Saints, New, and with many more Saints and the Passion . . ." *Der heiligen leben nüw mit vil me Heiligen, und darzu der Passion* . . . published by Grüninger, with Brant's collaboration, in 1502. From any point of view it is a de luxe edition, richly illustrated. One illustration, representing a man offering an open book to the Virgin Mary, is superscribed "S. Brand." Another shows a panorama of Strasbourg, one of the oldest in existence. Another edition by Grüninger is dated 1510, but a revised 1513 redaction bears the name of Hupfuff, and a still later one, of 1521, was printed by Martin Flach for Johann Knoblouch.

Another printer for whom Brant worked during his early years in Strasbourg was Johannes Wehinger, who commissioned him in 1502 to translate a so-called *Hortulus animae* ("Garden of the soul"), a popular breviary, into German (but see Zarncke, p. 172). The following lines are taken from the rhymed title: "Zu Straszburg in seym vatterland/hat mich Sebastianus Brant/besehenn [revised] und vast corrigiert/zu tütschen [into German] ouch vil transferiert,/mich druckt [printed] Johannes Wähinger. . . ." An edition of 1504 was again printed by Wehinger; later redactions were done by other printers elsewhere, but the evidence is not clear whether Brant had a hand in these.

Working for Grüninger, Brant edited *Virgilii opera* in 1503, richly illustrated with over two hundred cuts,[18] but weighted down with the commentaries of Servius, Donatus, and several Italian scholars. An older Nuremberg edition was used as the basis. The edition is marred by its emphasis upon works then falsely attributed to Virgil. They are all included—among them *Culex, Ciris,* and *Moretum*—with synopses, but with a warning about *Priapus*, which, as we saw, was too lewd for Brant's taste. Virgil, to whom Heynlin had called his special attention, always remained one of Brant's favorite poets. Chapter 112 of the *Narrenschiff* is for the most part a free translation of the poem *Vir bonus*, which Brant counted among the genuine works of Virgil.

A year later he also re-edited the comedies of Terence for Grüninger, who had previously published two inferior editions. This undertaking is not to be confused with the translation of

Terence not by Brant, referred to in Chapter 2. Brant proved in his new redaction that Terence's plays were not written in prose, but in a meter peculiar to the *carmina comica*. In proceeding to illustrate this he goes to pedantic extremes, quoting one ancient poet after another to prove his point. He voices no significant protest against the animal spirits displayed by Terence. Nor does he, on the other hand, in alluding to Hrotsvit's *comica sancta* ("religious comedies"), make a point of the Gandersheim nun's desire to replace Terence's pagan plays with Christian dramas. He shows more tolerance toward, and understanding for, Humanism than did Wimpheling. Yet in these editions of Classical Latin writers he was no match for his student Locher, whose edition of Horace (1498) in particular was epoch-making.

A "Geographical Description of Parts of Germany, its Waterways, Mountains, Towns, and Frontiers, with special attention to Alsace and 'the worthy city of Strasbourg'" (*Beschreibung etlicher Gelegenheit Teutsches landes, an wasser, berg, steten und grenzen* . . .),[19] was compiled by Brant some time during his residence there, probably not many years after his arrival. It was not published during his lifetime, but in 1539 it appeared as a supplement to Caspar Hedio's *Ein auserlesene Chronik von Anfang der Welt bis auf das Jahr 1539* ("A choice chronicle from the beginning of the world to 1539"), published in Strasbourg by Crafft Myller. Hedio's work is a translation of a much earlier Latin treatise. Another product of this time, the exact date of which is not known, is a work designated as *Freiheitstafel* ("Tablet of freedom"). It was discovered in the seventeenth century by Theophilus Dachtler (known also by his Humanist name of Elychnius), a secretary in the Strasbourg government, who will be mentioned again later in connection with Brant's so-called Epigrams. Dachtler probably made the existing copy from the original, which has disappeared.[20] Strobel printed it for the first time in his edition of the *Narrenschiff* (1839).

The work is a collection of fifty-three short German strophes which Brant composed at various times, describing, in a moralizing vein, the murals in one of the meeting rooms of the Strasbourg city hall, reserved for the College of Thirteen, a sort of municipal supreme court. Brant's didactic comments reflect the spirit of freedom enjoyed by the good burghers of the free and imperial city. No. 27 may serve as an example. The mural represents a naked child with a dagger in its hand. Brant's verses read: "Emperor Julius was generous and righteous,/but when he deemed Rome his slave/and wanted to be master alone,/as though there were no more freedom,/terrible vengeance was taken upon him for that:/he was stabbed to death with many wounds." [21]

Another important document from the pen of Brant, preserved in Strasbourg in a copy made after his death, is his lengthy and graphic German report on the election and solemn entry into the city of the newly chosen bishop Wilhelm von Hoenstein in 1506, and 1507, respectively. It is entitled *Bischoff Wilhelms von Hoensteins waal und einrit.*

The scion of a prominent Thuringian family, the bishop made his festive entrance early in the autumn of 1507, accompanied by many nobles and high officials. Extreme precautions had been taken by the city government to insure law and order. Brant describes the arrangements and the march in detail, narrating how the cathedral was cleared of crowds of people "by force and with sticks" (*mit gewalt und mit stecken*), and how the new bishop refused to march under a baldachin, preferring to walk among the cuirassiers, "of whom he was more worthy." Noting the fact that the city councilmen, invited to a banquet by the bishop, were poorly served, he remarks humorously that there was more to see than to eat. He is also frank to confess that there is reason for doubting the lasting good will of the prelate toward the townsfolk. But he praised Von Hoenstein for being the first bishop in over one hundred and fifty years to sing a mass in person in the cathedral. "Most bishops were too haughty," he remarks, "and left such offices to their subordinates."

It was a characteristic of Brant that after having published a certain type of work he was occasionally tempted to write another that might be considered a parallel to the first. His legal textbook *Expositiones sive declarationes* . . . of 1490 was followed ten years later by his edition of Gazalupis' *De modo studendi.* . . . And his *Narrenschiff* was succeeded in 1508 by an edition of a collection of gnomic verse in the form of epigrams, the work of a Swabian poet who lived in the thirteenth century and wrote under the assumed name of Freidank. Called *Beschei-*

denheit, in the old connotation of "prudence" or "sagacity," it was printed by Grüninger.

This book has much in common with the *Narrenschiff*, abounding in versified proverbial and aphoristic sayings. Like the *Narrenschiff*, it has much to say about fools: the world needs fools as well as wise men; fools copy new styles and customs from each other; they are complacent; a man who deems himself wise has all the earmarks of a fool; one wise man's courage is worth all the possessions of two fools. Brant added many supporting quotations from the Bible and from the ancients, and explained difficult passages.

There are forty-six rather inferior cuts. Hans Schönsberger printed a new edition in Augsburg in 1510. Later editions, especially those published in Worms in 1538 and 1539, contain some of the same cuts but otherwise have nothing to do with Brant's first edition of this work. But it is doubtful if Brant took the trouble to read the proofs, for the slender quarto volume abounds in misprints. Nevertheless it is important in revealing an interest, on Brant's part, in native vernacular literature of an earlier period. Such interest is a rare phenomenon among the Humanist writers of his age.

There is yet another group of shorter German poems by Brant, the date of which is uncertain but most if not all of which originated during the Strasbourg years. Copies of these, now known as epigrams, had been made by Dachtler, mentioned above in connection with the *Freiheitstafel*. In a Strasbourg manuscript compiled by Jacob Wenker, the author of the first article on Brant to appear in the eighteenth century,[22] these poems, seventy-seven in number, were transcribed from copies made from Dachtler's manuscript. Strobel [23] had published some of them, but Zarncke[24] was the first to print them all.

Some of these epigrams are headed by Latin quotations from the Old Testament or from Latin authors. These serve as themes for the epigrams themselves, like the mottos of the *Narrenschiff*. One gains the impression that this collection, in a moralizing vein, could serve as a supplement to Freidank's work, as well as to the *Narrenschiff*. Indeed, passages occur that are little more than echoes of Freidank[25] and of the *Narrenschiff*.[26] Occasionally

Brant borrows ideas from Tengler's *Layen Spiegel,* to be discussed below.

The *Esel* ("ass"), *Gouch* ("cuckoo"), and *Narr* are mentioned not infrequently. Zarncke's No. 46 (p. 158) may serve as a typical example and will show how closely related in spirit these epigrams are to the *Narrenschiff:* "Whoever despises all the world ostentatiously/and boasts of his nobility mightily,/and ignores where he came from,/he is despised by all the world/because he is a fool day and night./ Many a goose has cackled." [27]

If we consider this group of epigrams as a single work—and it is usually so considered—and compare it not only with the *Narrenschiff* and Freidank, but also with *Fuchshatz,* we may speak of a quartet of parallel works representing a single type, in which satire, humor, and aphoristic comments on men and their manners play a major role.

There is another pair of parallel works, these appearing within seven years of one another. One is *Layen Spiegel: Von rechtmässigen ordnungen in Bürgerlichen und peinlichen regimenten* ("Mirror for laymen: Of legal provisions in civil and penal cases"), printed in 1509 by Hans Otmar in Augsburg. The other is *Der richterlich Clagspiegel* ("Mirror of juridical lawsuits"), published in 1516 by Hupfuff in Strasbourg. But neither is an original work of Brant. The former, by Ulrich Tengler, whom Brant met through Locher, was provided with German prefaces by Brant, one in heavy German prose, the other in German verse. At Brant's urging two Latin prefaces, one in prose, the other in verse, were supplied by Locher, even though by 1509 Brant was no longer on good terms with his former student. Numerous later editions appeared between 1510 and 1560, most of them in Strasbourg.

The other book, the *Clagspiegel,* is by an unknown author whose original work may have appeared as early as 1470. Brant's *Clagspiegel* seems to be a new edition of a volume that had come out in 1497 under the title *Ein neu geteutscht Rechtbuch* ("A new law book turned into German"). It covers civil and canon law and offers practical instruction on how cases should be presented in court and decisions rendered. Brant revised the text, made corrections, and added about fifty lines of verse, in which he explains that he endeavored to turn Latin terms and expressions into German, so that they might be generally understood. He dedicated the volume to two Strasbourg councilmen. Numerous new editions appeared between 1518 and 1600.[28]

Frequent mention has been made of the many broadsides, laudatory poems, and pleas of one kind or another which Brant addressed to Emperor Maximilian. The earliest of them, it was found, date from soon after the ruler's election to the Roman kingship in 1486. From that time on, Brant never tired of addressing Maximilian, whose favor he had gained at an early date, for the purpose of urging him to act in uniting the German princes, regaining the Holy Land for Christianity, checking the inroads of the Turks, and enhancing the prestige of the Empire. He harbored the illusion that somehow Maximilian, as the temporal head of the Holy Roman Empire, occupied a position of leadership among all the Christian rulers of the known world.

By no means did Brant cease these importunities after his ambitious *De origine et conversatione* . . . in 1495. More than a dozen of the ninety-odd poems in his *Varia Carmina* come under this heading. After he left Basel, their number, far from decreasing, grew. Zarncke (pp. 197ff.) selects about half a dozen from among the numerous examples. Some of these laudatory effusions border on the ridiculous, as when he sings: "Whatever great gifts the gods may have given others throughout ancient times,/he [Maximilian] possesses them all by himself." [29] In another poem, the Emperor is told that all the heroes combined from Hercules and Hector to Alexander, and down to Charlemagne and Otto the Great can barely match him. As late as February, 1518, less than a year before Maximilian's death, Brant composed a poem "Ad divum Maximilianum Caesarem invictissimum," urging him to campaign against the Turks. The ruler's death called forth sixteen sonorous distichs, constituting what Brant called an "Epicedion." It ends in a prayer to God to assign the monarch a place "among the immortals above" (*apud superos*).

Maximilian's successor, Charles V, with whom a delegation headed by Brant had an audience in Ghent during the summer of 1520, was lauded by Brant in a lengthy German poem during August of that year.[30] It was probably composed not long before the gloomy lines on the plight of the Empire quoted in Chapter

2, where Brant prayed: "May God help holy Christianity! . . . May God will it that no deluge may come which will devour the whole earth. . . ." The tactful verses to Charles V, much more hopeful but probably not as sincere, reveal no trace of such pessimism.

CHAPTER 7

Brant, the Writer, Humanist, and Man: A Summary

I The Writer

AS the title indicates, this chapter summarizes the contents of the preceding pages insofar as they refer to the principal aspects of Brant's views and works, and endeavors to find the proper place for him in literary history. Therefore it restates, and occasionally elaborates upon what has been said before at various points of the discussion. The salient facts are tied together and brought into perspective in order to serve the purpose of a summary.

It would be difficult to find a writer during the last five hundred years who has been so grossly misinterpreted as Brant. Ever since serious study of him was begun by Zarncke in 1854, misconceptions have been numerous. One of the most serious concerns his masterpiece, the *Narrenschiff* (the only one of his numerous works singled out by scholars for close study). It was condemned for its lack of any consistent idea and its complete formlessness. M. O'C Walshe's recent utterance, which even distorts his intention, is typical of this reaction: "In the *Narrenschiff* Brant showed himself totally incapable of organizing a narrative event to the extent of maintaining the most elementary consistency in the story." [1]

I was one of the first to give Brant more credit. In 1945 I asked "whether the *Narrenschiff* . . . does not deserve a little more consideration as a work of literature." [2] Now, thanks to the research of Gaier, we are learning that Hutten was right when he lauded Brant for writing German poetry according to a new set of rules. In form as well as content, the *Narrenschiff* is seen to be a well-planned, consistently executed work deserving the praise of Brant's contemporaries. Its importance as a satire of late fifteenth-century life, skilfully constructed in the Roman style, in accordance with the rules of Roman rhetoric, can hardly be overestimated. In everyday language and striking pictures it showed the people the danger of their folly and endeavored to bring them to their senses and to the right mode of living, so as to save them, the Empire, and the Christian faith from destruction. It is one of the notable literary achievements of its time. Gaier thinks that critics have overlooked the unique quality of the German version as opposed to Locher's Latin version. The original German assigns a *religious* aspect to folly, based upon a concept of harmony missing in Locher. Brant's "wise man" (*wis man*) is conceived as a microcosmic image of the divine, and his qualities as such may some day impregnate his environment—with the attendant destruction of folly. In no other pre-Renaissance work can such a world view be found.

After more than a hundred years of misjudgment a Brant revival seems to be taking place. Zeydel's only English translation has proved popular, as two new editions attest. Lemmer's new redaction of the original and his publication of the woodcuts, Gaier's novel approach, and Wuttke's plans for an edition of the letters and other works are indications of this trend. Literary criticism in general must follow.

It is a natural impression today that the *Narrenschiff* was the only work of Brant to achieve marked success. On the contrary, many of his writings attracted wide interest in their day, even those in Latin. His early legal textbooks, as well as his edition of Gazalupis, went through numerous printings and revisions over a period of more than one hundred years, attracting printers as far away as Paris, Lyons, and Venice. His German translation of the Latin *Cato* was reprinted well over a dozen times within some twenty years, as was the equally popular *Facetus,* which by 1518 was known through local editions in Reutlingen, Ulm, Augsburg, Nuremberg, and Leipzig. The *Varia Carmina* proved so popular that within three months of the appearance of the original Basel edition Grüninger published a pirated edition in Strasbourg. Brant's Latin redaction of Aesop, the German *Layen Spiegel,* and the "Lives of the Saints," as well as the *Hortus Animae* mostly in German, enjoyed equal popularity.

It is to be noted that of the eleven works just mentioned only five are entirely in Latin; the rest are in German. In view especially of the overwhelming popularity of the *Narrenschiff* in High and Low German, as well as of *Cato* and *Facetus,* we may judge that Brant was far better known, in Central Europe at least, as a German author than as a Latinist.

All of Brant's works enjoyed a measure of success in their day. But he was less successful in a number of his writings of the type known as *suasoria*—the suasive writings. To this category belong the many broadsides aimed at arousing the Emperor and the princes to action against the Turks and in the Holy Land, the still more numerous eulogistic poems addressed to Maximilian and animated by the same burning desire, as well as the treatise *De origine et conversatione*. . . . These products of Brant's pen served to show where he stood on matters of imperial foreign policy; but they hardly succeeded in spurring Maximilian, not to mention the princes, to deeds. Although it is true that Brant enjoyed the favor of his monarch, his eloquence could not supply the manpower or the funds to undertake a campaign as costly as a holy war.

The fact that the broadsides are usually composed in both Latin and German indicates that Brant was interested in reaching wider circles. His aim was probably to make such a holy war a popular cause. Since all the broadsides, and even many of the longer Latin writings, among them *De origine et conversatione* . . . , and Aesop, were accompanied by woodcut illustrations, we can be sure not only that Basel was well supplied with facilities for such work, but also that Brant hoped to appeal to as many people as possible regardless of language or literacy. Even the appearance of a German translation of *De origine et conversatione* . . . twenty-three years after the original Latin edition has some significance, although Brant probably had little or nothing to do with the belated publication by a Swiss translator. It appeared in Strasbourg under the imprint of a publisher with whom Brant had worked.

II *The Humanist*

Now if Brant's literary success was attributable more to his German than to his Latin writings, how can he be classed with the Humanists, who were certainly not known for works in the vernacular? Before answering this question, it is necessary to examine German Humanism during Brant's lifetime, and his attitude toward it.

Humanism had, of course, been born in Italy as early as the fourteenth century and had developed to a considerable extent before being brought north. It did not take root in Germany until about the time of Brant's youth, shortly after the middle of the fifteenth century.

Three main factors seem to have influenced early German Humanism, especially that of Alsace, and given it direction. These factors are: (1) The new religion of *devotio moderna,* which came from the Netherlands and was introduced by the schoolman Dringenberg in Schlettstadt. (2) As a corollary to this, the Nominalist-Realist quarrel, especially Heynlin's Realist role in it. (3) The Latin prose works of Petrarch, whom Brant admired and some of whose works he edited.

Devotio moderna, closely related to *docta ignorantia,* came to the German Humanists especially from Nicolaus Cusanus, one of the key figures of the Basel Church Council, the decrees of which Brant had edited in 1499. Heynlin practiced it, and Brant learned it from him. An idea of its nature can be had from some of its tenets, such as: "happy [is] simplicity which leaves the difficult paths of problems, and walks on the plain and firm road of the commandments of God" (*beata simplicitas quae difficiles quaestionum relinquit vias et plana ac firma pergit semita mandatorum Dei*); or "beware then, son, of dealing curiously with these matters that transcend your knowledge" (*cave ergo, fili, de istis curiose tractare quae tuam scientiam excedunt*); or "grace teaches . . . that we seek of everything and in all knowledge the fruit of what is useful, and the praise and honor of God" (*gratia docet . . . de omni re et in omni scientia utilitatis fructum atque Dei laudem et honorem quaerere*); or finally "human reason is weak and can err, but true faith cannot be wrong" (*ratio humana debilis est et falli potest, fides autem vera falli non potest*).[3]

Here is the root of that refusal to deal in speculative philosophy in which Brant and the other early German Humanists, particularly those who opposed Nominalism, like Heynlin, joined. *Docta ignorantia* and its religious offshoot, with their symbolic blending of theism and pantheism, or, as Stadelmann (p. 74) puts it, "concave mysticism," became a hallmark of Alsatian Humanism.

The attraction to Petrarch that Brant felt, and Petrarch's impact upon him have already been mentioned. As we saw, Brant edited several of his Latin prose works. But coming to his notice somewhat later in life, Petrarch exercised less influence in initiating Brant's Humanism than he did in giving that Humanism purpose and enthusiastic determination.

In the north, the Italian character of Humanism changed, in part at least because of a different attitude toward the Classics. In Italy they (the Latin Classics in particular) were looked upon as a natural indigenous heritage, whereas in the northern countries they represented a foreign importation, a supplement to native traditions.

In Italy Humanism was regarded as an educational ideal, and Humanist learning as an end in itself, an aristocratic but sometimes frivolous ornament that was meant to lend distinction to the scholar. In the north, however, and in Germany in particular, Humanism served—at least at first—not as an end, but as a means of revealing new horizons and, more important, of living a more pious life by achieving a better understanding of one's faith. The German brand, too, proved more democratic than its Italian counterpart. Whereas the Italian Humanist, for instance, combed the monasteries of Europe for Classical manuscripts, his German colleague showed more interest in the new art of printing, to the end that knowledge might be disseminated through books.

In spite of these differences, however, the impact of Italian Humanism upon Germany is undeniable. To realize it, we must turn to such a famous Italian Humanist as Laurentius Valla (Lorenzo della Valle), who died in the year Brant was born. He opposed the hegemony of the old traditional disciplines. In his *De voluptate,* the German Humanist could find the bases for the protest against lax morals voiced by Heynlin and Brant; in *Elegantiae Latini Sermonis* encouragement for their endeavor to write better Latin. Like Reuchlin and Brant, Valla had reservations about jurisprudence.

There can be no question that Brant had enjoyed good training in Latin before he left home in 1475, although Reuchlin, his senior by two years, and Erasmus, some nine years younger, possessed a better knowledge of the Classics and a deeper appreciation of their ideals. Partly owing to Heynlin's influence, he devoted much time to both Latin and Greek during his early years in Basel, Reuchlin being one of his teachers, with perhaps the decisive influence on him in the direction of Humanism. The disparaging, biting remarks about Brant's Latin made by an anonymous correspondent in 1480 and quoted in Chapter 1, should not be taken seriously. We must also be cautious in interpreting Brant's reply to him when he writes: "I never said that I was a poet; I am not even a student of poetry." [4] Brant must be interpreted merely as saying that by 1480 he had become immersed in the study of law. It does not signify that he had abandoned the Classics, Latin or Greek.

In time he became better versed, even in Greek, than is generally realized. He was secretly proud of his Latin. It can be seen that he resents the same anonymous writer's slur on his "crude" Latin poems and would leave their criticism to others (*id aliorum relinqui judicio*). He also criticizes the Latin of his correspondent, who "writes a barbarous style" (*usque adeo barbaras*); "of little eloquence" (*eloquentiae parvae*); "so that it seems like stupid babbling" (*ut balbutientes ineptire videantur*). Locher, we found, was enthusiastic about Brant's teaching of the Latin classics in 1487—an activity which apparently continued (perhaps desultorily) even after 1496. And, we recall, Brant edited Virgil and Terence.

He was born into the first generation of German Humanism. And indeed he reveals the limitations of that generation insofar as Humanism is concerned. These also characterize his friend Wimpheling, who was about seven years his senior. Wimpheling, too, was an ardent advocate of Latin. Unlike Brant, he wrote almost *all* his works, over fifty in number, in that tongue. Whenever the opportunity offered, he advocated the use of Latin in serious writing. This becomes manifest in such major educational writings as *Adolescentia, De integritate,* and *Diatriba.* But Wimpheling's reasons for studying Latin and using it as a means of communication were typical of his generation. He aimed thereby to be able to enjoy free interchange of ideas with other clerics throughout Europe, to have full access to the Vulgate

Bible and the writings of the Church fathers, and thus to become a better Christian.

The question naturally arises why Wimpheling did not then limit his studies to Christian sources, instead of going back to some of the Classical writers of Roman times? His answer was: Because they wrote a purer Latin style than the later writers (especially the Scholastics) had cultivated. And besides, poets like Virgil and philosophers like Seneca, standing on the threshold of the Christian era, possessed in his view traits that were not un-Christian and that opened new vistas. But he abhorred paganism in any form and consequently rejected poets like Terence and Horace.

Reuchlin, also one of Brant's oldest, most steadfast friends, belongs to the same generation and shared the beliefs common to the early German Humanists. He had a better knowledge than Brant of the Classics, especially Greek, and a better appreciation of their real value. Like Brant he turned reluctantly from the Classics to law because he had scruples about jurisprudence, which he voiced in *De verbo mirifico*. Above all, he was a good Christian, and as did Wimpheling and Brant, had the purpose of helping and furthering the Church in everything he undertook. Brant admired Reuchlin for his erudition, his interest in the cabala of the Hebrews, as expressed in *De verbo mirifico*. He also looked up to him as a writer of comedy.

On the other hand, most of the early German Humanists, having special predilections, possessed a strong feeling of cultural nationalism, Brant in particular because he spent his life on the frontier of Germanic civilization. Some, among them Celtes and Tritheim, went so far as to forge history in order to enhance the ethnic and literary prestige of the Germanic peoples. Wimpheling opposed French territorial ambitions along the Rhine, especially in Alsace and northern Italy; and Brant pictured Emperor Maximilian as the master of the entire civilized Christian world and dreamed of a stronger constitution for Germany. He wanted to revive the Crusades and stir up more feeling against the Turks.

It is precisely this cultural nationalism that prompted Brant to write as much as he did in the vernacular. As was said before, he wanted to reach the masses and to convey to them the ideas that he and his Humanist friends cherished. Far from being against Humanism, Brant shared the motives of the other German Humanists, though he did not despise the pagan authors—not even Catullus or Terence. To a very limited degree, his striving can be compared with that of Luther and his followers, who in some respects subscribed to Humanism. In theology and religion Brant was, of course, diametrically opposed to Luther, but he, like Murner, agreed with Luther that it was essential to reach the people in their own tongue through the new art of the printing press.

To a certain extent Brant was perhaps still influenced by late Scholasticism in its blending of Church dogma with Aristotelian metaphysics, particularly as regards the treatment of form and matter, *actus* and *potentia*. But this influence is not pervasive. Already during his youth Scholasticism and its schools were breaking down. The quarrel between Nominalists and Realists had been carried on in dead earnest by the Scholastics. But exceptionally Brant, the Realist, felt friendly toward and even intimate with such Nominalists as Hugonis and Reuchlin. And he and his associates never shared the Scholastic addiction to logic and logomachy.

On the whole Brant was a representative, though not in all respects a typical one, of early German Humanism. He was an enthusiastic student and teacher of the Classics. He edited the writings of two Roman authors. As Humanists were supposed to do, he composed Latin poetry. He was notably active in printing, publishing, and editing. He was at least interested in the voyages of Columbus and actively engaged in the study of geography, a Humanist occupation which he shared with Celtes and Pirckheimer. He strongly advocated cultural nationalism. A devout Christian and adherent of the old faith, he wrote tirelessly in the vernacular to enlighten the common folk in these matters. He was no less active in impressing his political philosophy upon the people.

The generation of Humanists that succeeded Brant, represented by his pupil Locher and by Heinrich Bebel, blazed new trails. They strongly advocated better Classical Latin in speech and writing, a goal which Brant, in Valla's tradition, vaguely strove for. More important, as we have seen, they urged the study of the Latin language, so that the Classics might be read for their own enjoyment and for the sake of endowing man's spirit with new freedom. This point of view aroused the suspicion and hostility of some members of the older generation because it was considered un-Christian. This helps to explain Brant's later coolness toward his favorite pupil and Wimpheling's dislike of that "apostate."

III *Outstanding Characteristics of Brant*

In the course of our discussion one characteristic of Brant was stressed—his concern to adjust his language to the cultural level of the audience being addressed. Here a bilingual writer like Brant, audience-conscious as he was, faced problems of which present-day writers can hardly be aware. He tells each audience just what he feels it could and should know. The German readers of the *Narrenschiff*, for instance, to whom he stresses religion, are not given all the political and historical reasons why he must admonish them. They are told that folly leads to perdition, but that the wise man, deriving his wisdom from heaven, may gradually displace the fool. The fear of the possible downfall of the Empire through folly and lack of *ordo* is largely reserved for the Latin readers of his prefaces to Locher's translation and his poem "De corrupto ordine vivendi. . . ."

Another feature of Brant is his keen sense of form and of the rules of rhetoric. This explains his success with the Roman type of satire in the *Narrenschiff*, as well as his skilful handling of the historical events (as he saw them) in the treatise *De origine et conversatione* . . . and in the poem "De corrupto ordine vivendi. . . ."

Turning from purely formalistic and stylistic matters to questions of content, and looking at Brant's works as a whole, one is surprised to find remarkable uniformity of theme. A topical list of the subjects and views aired by him can be boiled down to a few headings, most of which are somehow related or contiguous. The reason for this is not difficult to find. To Brant religion, politics, and publicistic activity were all expressions or manifestations of a single world view which to Brant was a matter of life and death.

By and large Brant's principal thesis, though not infrequently

[130]

only implied, is the hegemony of the Church, the inviolability of Church dogma, and a deep love for the Virgin Mary, together with a firm belief in the immaculate conception. The corollary, no less important, is the position of the Empire in the temporal world, not on a par with, but immediately below, the Church. The Pope takes the highest place in the hierarchy of rulers, the Emperor the second place. Equally important is the leadership, among nations, of the German people as the subjects of this Empire, which takes precedence over all other bodies politic. The important role played by Brant's teachers Heynlin, Von Andlau, and Hugonis in inculcating these convictions should be borne in mind.

Leaving the ecclesiastical and purely political scene, we note that Brant is no less concerned with the morals and manners of the people. He decries their lack of wisdom and their cultivation of folly, fearing that these may contribute to the decline of the Christian faith and to the loss of temporal world leadership on the part of the German nation. Moral teaching, supported by satire, and attention to the lessons of the Bible, the ancient writers, and history are the best means of overcoming these faults. Brant constantly reminds his audience that even foibles and idiosyncrasies will lead to worse errors. One of the best means of disseminating truth is through books; indeed, that is to his mind the chief virtue of the new art of printing.

As for Humanism, Brant's commitment had become so strong in his mature years that he went to extremes to train his son Onuphrius as a Humanist. And unwittingly his teaching of the Classics contributed in a positive way to the rearing of the more liberal generation of Humanists represented by Locher.

Again and again Brant stressed his fear that the end of the world—the Christian world as he knew it—was close at hand; sometimes he even feared that the whole world would be destroyed. It might come, he thought, through natural causes, as the result of a great disaster, often foreboded by such phenomena as floods, storms, or meteors. Or it might result from further inroads of the Turks. He believed every prophet of doom. This prompted him to urge the Emperor repeatedly to wage a holy war, or to initiate a crusade for the reconquest of the Holy Land.

The keynote, then, of Brant's attitude toward the world is not contempt but concern for it, and a burning desire to teach people to live in it more wisely.

However, we must not overlook some inconsistencies in Brant's world picture. Though worried about the state of the world, he is on the whole an advocate of the status quo. He is deeply interested in history but, like many of his contemporaries, he is devoid of historical perspective. He was a notorious Germanophile but was looked upon in Strasbourg as *romanissimus*—quite Gallic. Though a Humanist, he avoided some of his confreres in later life, among them Locher and even Reuchlin. His stand with regard to superstition is equivocal.[5]

The question of Brant's feeling with respect to the unrest in the Church caused by the activity of Luther and his adherents has been referred to. In dealing with this it must be recalled that in his official position in Strasbourg he was never entirely free to express his personal opinion. Moreover, the Lutheran Reformation, or Revolt—whichever term one may prefer—had at the time of Brant's death not brought about a full break with the Mother Church, although most signs pointed in that direction. Although Brant probably saw the handwriting on the wall, he expressed only vague fears of what might happen. To some this was not enough. Murner, for instance, who during Brant's last days was turning ever more against Luther, censured his friend for not taking a firm enough stand against the enemies of the Church.

As for Luther himself, actually only one point of agreement between him and Brant has been noted: they both wanted to reach the people through the vernacular. There the similarity ends. One thing is certain, however. Brant's philosophy, religious and political, told him that Lutheranism was bound to spell disaster for every ideal and hope he cherished.

It should be remembered that Brant was not prone to reason about religious convictions. The aversion to philosophical speculation, which through Cusanus Heynlin had instilled in him, was one of his outstanding characteristics. Like Heynlin, he limited himself to everyday morality, Humanistic education, and practical religiosity. His thinking in these matters is perhaps most clearly expressed in the first of his epigrams: "Do not allow yourself to be led astray from the faith/if someone wants to argue about it./ Rather believe plainly and simply/as the Holy Church teaches you./ Do not accept the overly subtle doctrine/that your reason cannot understand./ The little sheep often floats to the shore/ where the elephant has trouble and drowns./ No one should ask too many questions/about his faith or his wife;/then in the end he will have no regrets." [6]

This humble advice—*docta ignorantia*—describes Brant's position on matters of faith and stamps him as a stanch adherent of orthodoxy. He had been adverse to new, unorthodox teachings as early as 1494, when he wrote his *Narrenschiff*. A passage in Chapter 11 of that work, which sounds almost prophetic in the light of what happened some twenty-five years later, runs:

> I fear the day is near when you
> Will hear new teachings, new belief,
> Far more than pleasing, more than lief . . .[7]

But it was too late. Brant was powerless to set back the clock. The lament written shortly before his death, and quoted in Chapter 2, that great changes will occur in fruit, fish, birds, beast, and men was only too well founded, at least so far as men were concerned.

Although his beloved Onuphrius, the precocious son of a learned father, was reared in the only traditions that his sire could comprehend, he must have been more strongly exposed and more susceptible to the changes affecting the religious life of wide areas of northern Europe. Not many years after his father's death, Onuphrius declared his adherence to Protestantism.

Notes and References

Chapter One

1. It was common practice among Humanistic writers, especially of the fifteenth and sixteenth centuries, to use Latin or Greek adaptations or translations of their names, particularly as authors of Latin writings. Thus Bauer became Agricola; Müller, Molitor; Becker, Pistor, etc. Schwarzerd was turned into Melanchthon (Greek for "black earth"), a misconception of the etymology of the German name, and Reuchlin into Kapnion (Greek for "smoke"). An amusing example is that of the Polish Humanist Nicholas Vodka, who called himself Abstemius. See Leonard Foster, *Selections from Conrad Celtis* (Cambridge, 1948), p. 4, n. In *Götz von Berlichingen*, Goethe alludes pointedly to this practice. The first example I know of, however, is of a much earlier date. Hrostvit in the tenth century, translating her name (Hruot svinth), speaks playfully of herself as *ego clamor validus* ("I, the loud noise").

2. The badly preserved inscription reads: "Sebastiano Brant Argentino U.J. Doctori, Poetae ac Oratori Disertissimo, Hujus Urbis Archigramateo, Sacri Caesarei Palatii Comiti Aequissimo Hic Sepulto. Hoc Marmor Intuens Coelos Optato. Vixit An. LXIIII. Obiit Anno MDXXI. Die X Men. Maji. Omnia Mors Aequat." ("To Sebastian Brant of Strasbourg, doctor of both laws, most learned poet and orator, arch-chancellor of this city, most righteous Imperial Count Palatine, buried here. In the face of this marble pray to Heaven. He lived sixty-four years. He died in the year 1521. On the tenth day of May. Death levels everything.")

3. See Jaro Springer, *Sebastian Brants Bildnisse*. Besides the work of Stimmer, the best likenesses are by Hans Burgkmair (1508) and Dürer, as well as those of the two Holbeins (one lost but preserved in a copy), and by Hans Baldung Grien, likewise preserved only in a copy. See also J. Janitsch, *Das Bildnis Brants von Albrecht Dürer*. Add to these the three woodcuts in which Brant is said to appear, in *Flugblätter des Sebastian Brant* edited by Paul Heitz. The cut in Berg-

mann's edition of the *Varia Carmina* (1498) is also supposed to represent Brant. Janitsch conservatively estimates eight likenesses.

4. Strobel in his edition of the *Narrenschiff* gives 1458; Zarncke in his edition, 1458; Schmidt in *Histoire Littéraire,* 1457; Goedeke, 1457; Steinmeyer, 1458. It is to be noted that the tombstone inscription says he *lived* sixty-four years.

5. On this famous letter see *Archiv für Kunde österreichischer Geschichtsquellen herausgegeben von der* . . . , Commission der kaiserlichen Akademie der Wissenschaften, XVI, 1856 (No. 482), 416.

6. "Ego fortunam ipsam fugientem moror, sequerer fortassis, nisi ipsa rerum dispensatrix nollet. Sed quod grataris mihi, quoniam pro singulis versibus singulos byzantinos receperim; ita habeas velim mihi pergratam, immo jocundam esse suam istam εὐτραπελίαν. Plane spe futurae numerationis recepi. Vereor tamen ne jam unus et item alter annus obstabit petenti." Quoted by Strobel, p. 7. Some of the Reuchlin-Brant correspondence is published by Ludwig Geiger in *Johann Reuchlins Briefwechsel,* in *Bibliothek des litterarischen Vereins in Stuttgart,* vol. 126 (1875).

7. Bergmann states this in his preface to Brant's *Varia Carmina.* See note 25 below.

8. See Strobel, *op. cit.,* p. 4: "Ex rudibus particularibus scholis in hoc Basiliense gignasium [*sic!*] peragrasti." ("You came from inferior private schools to this 'gymnasium' in Basel").

9. "ab ineunte aetate." Quoted by Zarncke, *op. cit.,* p. xi.

10. See Strobel, p. 6: "Superos enim obtestor quum tibi, ut auguror, neque publice, neque privatim nocui unquam, sic neque de caetero nocebo, nisi lacessitus. Recognosce igitur paulum stultitiam tuam, et saltem verecundi hominis faciem sume, non semper officium tibi assumas sycophantae. Non sis semper mendax, detractor, convicator. Abjice quaeso deinceps haec omnia, quisque fueris me quam primum certiorem facito, id abs te impetratum iri percupio. Quod ubi feceris me tibi non amicum modo, verum etiam amicissimum existimes velim. Et profecto si voles omnibus officiis efficiam ut ita esse vere possis iudicare. Et de his hactenus satis superque. Gessi enim tibi morem qui litteras, uti mandaveras, ad te dedi, quem innominatum fore quem aegerrime fero, quas cum accipies, facies quod voles. Voles autem mutuam inter nos et familiaritatem et amicitiam quam libentissime si eum me esse cognoveris qui vere sum. . . ."

11. See Zarncke, p. xi: "Quod me admones: ut amiciciam quam ab ineunte aetate peperim: adolescens conservem in te adolescentem, quamquem eo te animo esse doleo: qui me in hac re exhortandum esse senseas: tamen non tam mihi molestum fuit: suspectum tibi esse amorem meum, quam iucundum requiri."

Notes and References

12. See Strobel, p. 3: "Caeteri fere omnes poetae habebant quos insectabantur, ut Virgilius Homerum, et Terencius Manandrum [sic!] et caeteri caeteros. Tu es tibi ipsi dux et praeses. Verbum forte non arbitraris rarum, nisi quod nusquam reperitur. Commisces graeca latinis, semigraecus es et semilatinus, in utraque lingua deficiens, in neutra integer. Habet illa tua pompa et mos quo te effers super caeteros, originem a te, te autore, et habet; quia non accepi te unquam apud eos fuisse praeceptores qui te usque adeo doctum in Humanitatis arte efficere quibant, uti te esse fulminas."

13. See Strobel, p. 5: "Sed quod mihi objicis arrogantiam, qua me vel poetam vel oratorem iactaverim. Loqueris tu quidem ut homines levissimi solent, qui quod eis innatum est vitium, aliis inpingere non verentur."

14. The copy of the poem I used in Strasbourg is not as corrupt as Strobel, p. 7, maintains.

15. *Narrenschiff*, Chapter 27, 11. 26ff.: "So sint wir zu Lyps, Erfordt, Wyen/ Zu Heidelberg, Mentz, Basel, gstanden,/ Kumen zu letst doch heym mit schanden. . . ." *Ibid.*, 11. 10ff.: "Das selb den meystern ouch gebrüst,/ Das sie der rehten kunst nit achten,/ Unnütz geschwetz alleyn betrachten,/ Ob es well tag syn, oder nacht,/ Ob hab ein mensch, eyn esel gmacht,/ Ob Sortes oder Plato louff,/ Sollch ler ist yetz der schulen kouff,/ Syndt das nit narren und gantz dumb,/ Die tag und nacht gant do mit umb/ Und krützigen sich und ander lüt. . . ." The English in the text is from Zeydel's translation.

16. The verses on Reuchlin are in Zarncke, p. 195. On Reuchlin see also Ludwig Geiger, *Johannes Reuchlin, sein Leben und seine Werke*, Leipzig, 1871. For the letter of Brant to Reuchlin see the Geiger edition of letters (note 6 above), pp. 48ff. Some papers and letters of Reuchlin in St. Gall are chiefly in Brant's hand. Among them is the address of Reuchlin to Brant's baccalaureate class. See p. 24 above. It is in Geiger's edition of Reuchlin's letters, pp. 340ff.

17. See Strobel, p. xiv (errata): "Quod praeterea scribis me intexere graeca latinis, inficior, qui heus neque graeca novi nisi prima elementa."

18. E.g., in his epigrams to Zasius against Locher. See Chapter 2, p. 58.

19. *In laudem gloriose virginis Marie multorumque sanctorum. Varii generis carmina Seb. Brant utriusque doctoris famosissimi*. 4⁰, 47 leaves.

20. On the Council of Basel see *Concilium Basiliense, Studien zur Geschichte des Conzils von Basel*, ed. by Johannes Haller, 8 vols., Basel, 1896–1936, especially vol. 5. Also C. C. Bernouilli, "Basels Bedeutung für Wissenschaft und Kunst im XV. Jahrhundert: Geistiges

Leben, Buchdruck" in *Festschrift zum 400. Geburtstage des ewigen Bundes zwischen Basel und der Eidgenossenschaft* (Basel, 1901), pp. 219–72, and William Gilbert's helpful typewritten dissertation. These few references are selected from among many touching upon the subject. This applies also to the references in notes 20–22. On Basel in general see *Geschichte der Stadt Basel* by Rudolf Wackernagel, especially II² (Basel, 1916).

21. On the Carthusian library in Basel see Bernouilli, *Basler Jahrbuch*, 1895, pp. 79ff; *Informatorium Bibliothecarii Carthusiensis*, ed. by Ludwig Sieber, Basel, 1888; Konrad Escher, *Die Miniaturen in den Basler Bibliotheken, Museen und Archiven*, Basel, 1917; James W. Thompson, *The Medieval Library*, Chicago, 1929; and Gilbert, *op. cit.*

22. See Bernouilli in *Basler Zeitschrift für Geschichte und Altertumskunde*, XII (1913), 53ff.; Ludwig Geiger, *Renaissance und Humanismus in Italien und Deutschland* (Berlin, 1882); K. R. Hagenbach in *Basler Neujahrblatt* (Basel, 1826); Peter Ochs, *Geschichte der Stadt und Landschaft Basel*, IV and V (Basel, 1819, 1821); Wilhelm Vischer, *Geschichte der Universität Basel von der Gründung 1460 bis zur Reformation 1529* (Basel, 1860); K. Thommen, "Die Rektoren der Universität Basel von 1460–1910" in *Festschrift zur Feier des 450 jährigen Bestehens der Universität Basel* (Basel, 1910), pp. 477ff.; also Gilbert, *op. cit.* In 1960, on the occasion of the 500th anniversary of the university, additional literature was published.

23. See Joseph Benzing in *Zentralblatt für Bibliothekswesen*, Beiheft 68 (1936); *Der Buchdruck des 15. Jahrhunderts. Eine bibliographische Übersicht*, herausgegeben von der Wiegendruck-Gesellschaft (Berlin, 1929–36); Karl Stehlin, *Regesten zur Geschichte des Buchdrucks bis zum Jahre 1500* in *Archiv für Geschichte des deutschen Buchhandels* XI (1888), 5–182; XII (1889), 6–70; L. F. T. Hein, *Repertorium Bibliographicum*, 4 vols. (Stuttgart and Paris, 1826–38); *Gesamtkatalog der Wiegendrucke;* Gilbert, *op. cit.* See also the Amerbach correspondence, ed. by Alfred Hartmann (Basel, 1942).

24. *Der Ritter vom Turn* was printed by Furter in 1493 (facsimile: Munich, 1922). Bergmann, at the time employed by Furter, got his training for the printing of Brant's *Narrenschiff* through it. As for Dürer's part in it see F. Winkler, *Dürer und die Illustrationen zum Narrenschiff*.

25. In a letter to Reuchlin of January 9, 1494, already cited in part in note 6 above, Brant admits that he gave up the Humanities reluctantly: "Ego a Musis in verbosas leges incidi" ("I have fallen from the Muses into the verbosity of the law"), *Bibliothek des litterarischen Vereins in Stuttgart*, vol. 126, p. 37. And in his preface to Brant's *Varia Carmina*, Bergmann writes to their mutual friend Wymmar von

Notes and References

Erkelenz: "Cogitur at juri nimis indulgere, scholisque atque fori strepitus iurgia vana sequi. Sic visum est superis: nulli Deus omnia soli contribuit, fati durus ubique tenor" ("But he is forced to engage in jurisprudence and to follow the vain noisy quarrels in school and at court. So it was willed by the gods. God gives no one man everything. Everywhere is the hard road of fate"). In a letter to Michael Windeck of January 16, 1499, Brant himself recalls that although he chose law, he never intended to abandon pure literary pursuits (See Schmidt, I, 195). But it would be erroneous to believe that he disliked law. As early as May 1, 1490, he wrote to Andreas Helmuth that jurisprudence was "heavenly." See also his letter to Johann Götz of March 7, 1499 (See Schmidt, I, 202).

26. See the retrospective letter to his friend Villinger of December 17, 1517. Curiously, he decided against it because, as he says, he shied away from any rule he would not have wished to violate. This letter is reprinted in *Jahresbericht des historischen Vereins von Schwaben und Neuburg*, 1851, p. 61.

27. Joseph Hürbin, *Peter von Andlau* (Strasbourg, 1897). Among his other professors of law were Surgant and Oiglin.

28. In the letter to Villinger (note 26 above), written when his wife was still alive, Brant makes the curious remark that he might wish a wife more pious, richer, better looking, and younger than himself. Obviously this was a jest. See Schmidt, I, 237. According to a notation in the St. Thomas archives, she died in March, 1527.

29. To Reuchlin he expressed the hope (on October 1, 1495), that Onuphrius, then eight or nine, would drink of the Castalian spring, like Reuchlin, and become Reuchlin's student (*Bibliothek des litterarischen Vereins in Stuttgart*, vol. 126, pp. 48ff.).

30. F. Fischer, *Johannes Heynlin genannt a Lapide* (Basel, 1851); Max Hossfeld in *Zentralblatt für Bibliothekswesen* XXV (1908), 161ff.; *ibid.*, *Basler Zeitschrift für Geschichte und Altertumskunde* VI (1907–1908), 309–56; VII (1908–1909), 79–219, 235–431. Also Tritheim, *De scriptoribus ecclesiasticis*, fol. 129b.

31. See Zarncke, p. 211: "Memini dulciter me puerum stipendiis felicis achademie sub te preceptore meruisse. O dulces confabulationes quas sermone tuo suauissimo conditas: publico in auditorio te profitentem accepimus. Auribus inquam tenellis et adhuc propter pubertatis mollitudinem strepentibus: Salutares ac beniuolas solite tue facundie disciplinas exhibuisti. Quotiens enim in frequenti gymnasio certamina poetarum grandisonamque veterum chelyn inflammasti? lepidoque susurro cantilenas orphicas, delphicasque permulsisti? quotiens ob Phoebi tui dexteritatem laureamque coronabilem, me ad Aganippidos vireta scaturientesque Castalii riuulos concitasti? Quemadmodum at-

tice iucunditatis princeps Demosthenes Platonisque nostri tenellus auditor, oratione quam Callistratus orator concitatissimus pro Oropo acturus ad eloquentie studium commotus extitit: Ita tu charissime praeceptor animum meum primitus ad foeliciores studiorum secessus: antraque iucundiora, tua affabilitate ac urbanitate induxisti. Gratias igitur non quas volumus sed quas nostri pectoris exiguitas valet: referre non dedignemur. Nam si gratiarum actiones in hoc epistolio pro infusa eloquentia: proque musarum inspiramine iam tibi persoluere conarer: Nilotici calami argutia: aegyptieque papyri crassitudo nostris sudoribus vix satis facerent."

32. Zarncke, p. 174: "Memor sum te crebro verbis quam honestissimis cum coram essem, nonnunquam etiam absentem scriptis solicitasse. quatenus singula Sebastiani Brant, quondam nostri conscholastici, carmina lucubrationesque tibi praeque omnibus uni transmitterem, quod eo libentius me facturum pollicebar, quo et tui et illius optimi viri sum observantissimus penitusque dicatus." ("I recall that often when I was present you urged me in most sincere words, and in letters when I was not there, that I should send you above all individual poems and studies of our fellow-student Seb. Brant, which I promised all the more gladly because I am an admirer of yours and of this excellent man, and deeply indebted to both").

33. W. Fraenger, *Altdeutsches Bilderbuch: Hans Weiditz und Sebastian Brant*, and P. Heitz, *Des Sebastian Brant Flugblätter* (with twenty-five illustrations).

34. The five works here mentioned can be found in Zarncke, pp. 131ff. The original *Facetus* is by Poggio. See also *Liber faceti docens mores hominum*, printed by Wolff in 1498 (Latin and German); *Reineri Phagifacetum, sive de facetia comedendi libellus, addita versione Sebastiani Brantii*, ed. by Hugo Lemcke, Stettin, 1880. Strobel, p. 74, refers to the latter under the title *De moribus et facetiis mense, translatum in teutonicum per Seb. Brant*, 1490. See also Carl Schroeder, *Der deutsche Facetus*.

35. *Studien zu den Passions- und Osterspielen des deutschen Mittelalters in ihrem Übergang vom Latein zur Volkssprache*, Berlin, 1963 (*Philologische Studien und Quellen*, vol. 18).

36. Indeed, intensive study of his handwriting as found in the Strasbourg municipal archives indicates that even his style of orthography in Latin is different from his German hand.

Chapter Two

1. The adjustment to new subject matter on the part of the middle class was made quickly. A generation after Brant, Hans Sachs had

already adapted himself to it. He, with others, broadened the horizon by including, besides history, the fruit of his reading in legend, folklore, and anecdote.

2. In a volume published by Bergmann in December, 1493, *Oratio Jasonis magni legati . . . in nuptias Maximiliani et Blancae Mariae* ("Oration of the great ambassador Jason . . . on the marriage of Maximilian and Blanca Maria"), there is a wedding poem by Brant celebrating "the happy and auspicious union," described as "the joining of a two-headed eagle and a man-eating serpent." The same work reappeared in Innsbruck in March of the next year, the actual date and place of the marriage, and may well have come to the attention of the young Emperor.

3. In his *Diatriba* (1514), Wimpheling lists only seventeen contemporary scholars trained entirely on Germanic soil, among them Brant and Geiler. All others he knew of had studied at least for a while in Italy or France. Brant was proud of his purely German training.

4. *Tractatus de canonica clericorum secularium vita* and, most important, *Libellus de Caesarea monarchia*. A new edition of the latter was published by Joseph Hürbin in the *Zeitschrift der Savigny-Stiftung für Rechtsgeschichte*, German. Abt., XII, 34–103, and XIII, 163–219.

5. See note 27, Chapter 1, also Gilbert, *The Culture of Basel*, pp. 196ff.

6. See Schmidt I, 51–53.

7. In Bern he concerned himself specifically with the morals of the local population and prevailed upon the magistracy to press its efforts to improve moral standards and principles among the people. See Gilbert, p. 231.

8. "Dar umb jnn grossem lob die ston,/ Die sich der welt hant abgethon/ Und synd durch gangen berg und tal,/ Das sie die welt nit bracht zu fal/ Und sie villicht verschuldten sich,/ Doch loszt die welt sie nit on stich,/ Wie wol sie nit verdienen kan,/ Das sie solch lüt sol by jr han."

9. "Wann man sicht eynen, der do will/Recht dun, und syn jnn wiszheyt styll,/ So spricht man, schow den duckelmuser,/ Er will alleyn syn eyn Carthuser/ Und tribt eyn apostützer stodt,/ Er will verzwifflen gantz an gott."

10. "Solt, wie er dut, dun yederman/ In der Chartusz die kutten an,/ Wer woltt die weltt dann fürbas meren,/ Wer wolt die lüt wysen, und leren,/ Es ist gotts will, noch meynnung nit,/ Das man der welt sich so abschütt/ Und uff sich selb alleyn hab acht,/ Solch red dunt narren tag, und nacht."

11. "Wann ich zwo selen hett jnn mir,/ Setzt ich lycht eyne den

gesellen für,/ Aber so ich hab eyn alleyn,/ So musz ich sorg han umb die eyn."

12. Quoted by Vischer, *Geschichte der Universität Basel von 1460–1529* (Basel, 1860), p. 165. See also Zeydel in *Modern Language Quarterly* IV, 210ff.

13. *Varia Carmina* 79: "Quid, Lapidane pater, potuit iucundius usquam/ Contigisse tamen laetius atque tibi,/ Quam quod totidem fallacis tempora saecli/ Aerumnasque graves sidera laetus adis./ Morte tua praesens te non timuisse profecto,/ Audivi mortem fatiferumque diem. . . . Proinde tibi in vita dederat Deus esse quieta/Tempora, apud superos iam meliora dabit; . . ./ Iudicio extremo testis tuus esse ciebor,/ Quem mortem amplexus sis bene sponte libens./ Hinc te, digne pater, precor in coelestibus aulis,/ Filiolo abjecti quod memor esse velis./ Sic tibi (quam meritus) contingat gloria, perpes/ Vita, salus, virtus, gaudia, laeta quies." (Zarncke, p. 191.)

14. On Geiler see Schmidt, I, 337–461.

15. *Ibid.*, I, 395.

16. *Ibid.*, I, 404.

17. "Tu mihi praeceptor, tu pater atque magister,/ Tu patriae nostrae gloria, fama, decor./ Te doctore parens nostra Argentina relucet. . . . Concio te plebis sequitur, tibi nomina ab inde/ Fausta tenes, plebis tu pater atque salus,/ Proinde tibi tribuat vitam Deus optimus illam/ Quam populum cunctum verbo opere atque doces." (Zarncke, p. 184).

18. The German was probably published separately; it reappeared in a pamphlet got out by Wimpheling. See Zarncke, pp. 154 and 195. Geiler's gravestone is in the Strasbourg cathedral. The Latin text of the four lines reads: "Quem merito deflet urbs Argentina, Ioannes/ Geilerus, Mons cui Caesaris est patria:/ Sede sub hac recubas, quam rexti Praeco fidelis,/ Sex prope lustra docens verba salutifera."

19. The broadside is entitled *Exhortatio contra perfidos et sacrilegos flamingos*. It is discussed in Chapter 3.

20. *Forschungen zur deutschen Theatergeschichte des Mittelalters und der Renaissance* (Berlin, 1914), pp. 343–45.

21. Leipzig and Zürich, 1932; pp. 343–45.

22. *Frühformen der deutschen Bühne*, Berlin, 1963 (Schriften der Gesellschaft für Theatergeschichte, Band 62), pp. 73ff.

23. To Reuchlin Brant writes on January 13, 1500, that he envies him his leisure among the Muses. See *Bibl. d. Litt. Vereins Stuttg.*, vol. 126, p. 64. Perhaps a serious illness of 1497, of which Schmidt (I, 214) speaks, was also a factor. In the letter just mentioned Brant jests that the rumor of his death was false.

24. Schmidt, I, 233.

25. Published by Strobel, p. 9: "ich wurd bericht, dasz man in willen syg von der Stadt einen andern *Doctor* uff zenemen. Hab ich gedacht an Dr. Brand [*sic*], der ein Kind von der Statt ist und fast wyt berümt in allen Landen für andern. Von der Kunst zeugen seine Geschrifften, was er kann in Tütsch und Latin. Er möcht auch alle Tag ein Stund lesen den Burgers Sünen und sie leren, das sie in frömden Landen mit grossen Kosten erholen müsten, und gieng alles in einem Sold zu. Dunkt mich auch der Statt erlich, dasz sie einen sollichen uss iren Burgern hetten und uss irer Statt bürtig, und nit einen frömden, auch ihm mer zu vertrawen wer. Mögend das ouch andren, wo euch das gut dunckt, zu verston geben als von uch selbs. Johann Kaisersperg."

26. She died December 6, 1506.

27. Strobel, pp. 9ff.: "In nächst verruckten Tagen, als ich in Geschäfften des Hochwürdigen mins Gnädigen Herrn von Basel abgevertiget, in uwer Statt Straszburg auch eine kleine Zit by miner Muter und Brüdern, mit denen etwas kurtzwerende ergetzlichkeit zu haben, enthalten, ist durch ettlich meiner Herrn und guten Gündern an mich gelangt, wie uwer strenge Wissheit bisshar einen *Doctorem* gehaben, des rattslag zu fuglichen Ziten in Rechtsübungen und Händeln gebrucht, der nun zu zitten von uwer ersamen Wissheit Urlop genommen und entpfangen, als ob ich understan solt an uwer fürsichtige Wissheit zu werben, ob dieselbe uwer allzit geerte Fürsichtigkeit, mich zu solchen Händeln annemmen und bestellen wolt, uff das ich solcher an mich gelangter Meynung sithar witter nochgedacht, in mitbetracht dass ich ein Kind uwer lobl. erentrichen Statt Strassburg byn, und noch alldo myn Muter, Brüder, und angeborner, auch sundergunstiger Herren und Fründ, ein eben mergliche Zal hab. . . . zu Hertzen auch genommen den Spruch des Keyserl. Rechtens: *Patria sua unicuique debet esse charissima*, einem jeden soll sin Vatterland das allerliebst syn, dann ouch dieselbe Lieb (als der Poet spricht) überträfflich alle Menschen zühet, und will nit in Vergässliheit gestellt sin. . . . So verr uwer ersame Wissheit zu willen syn würd, furter einen *Doctorem* anzunemmen, und noch zu ziten mit dheinem sich versehen, und aber ich zu solchen höchsten Fliss, uwer Strengkeit mit dienstbarlichem und geneigten Willen allzit, als minen Gnädigen Herren und Gebietern zu gehorsamen, und lieber zu dienen dann dheinen andern Fürsten, Herren oder Stätten, wöll uwer strenge Wissheit diss min Schriben in Gnaden und geneigtem Willen, inmassen von mir ussgegangen ist, vermerken."

28. Brant's friend Johann Wolf von Hermannsgrün congratulated him on January 9, 1504, on returning to a "Roman" town since he himself is *romanissimus*. Schmidt, I, 212.

29. *Politische Correspondenz der Stadt Strassburg im Zeitalter der Reformation* I, 1517–30, bearbeitet von *Hans Virck* (Strasbourg, 1882).

30. Strobel, p. 13, note 15: "Item, Stadtschreiber nit zu der Sachen oder in urteln reden, er werde dann gefragt."

31. *Ibid.*, p. 13, note 16: "ihn zu beschicken, früntlich mit ihm zu reden, ruwig zu sin."

32. This pension, however, was never actually paid, as Brant reports to Villinger in a letter of December 17, 1517. See Schmidt, I, 216. It was promised after Brant had penned a flattering distich imploring God to grant Maximilian the glory enjoyed by Trajan and Titus (a four-line German translation also exists). Later the distich appears in a German version (by Brant) of a Latin book on Vespasian presented to Charles V in 1520 by Onuphrius. See Zarncke, p. 173. On such effusive poems to Maximilian see below, Chapter 6.

33. *Contra judaeos et haereticos, conceptionem virginalem fuisse possibilem argumentatio* (124 lines). It appears in the *Varia Carmina*. See Zarncke, pp. 176ff.

34. "Unica semper avis Phoenix reparatur in igne,/ Sic vitam miseris unica virgo parit,/ Pennigeras volucres arbor producit Ibera,/ Quis vetat ut virgo parturit absque viro?" (Zarncke, p. 177).

35. The poem, also in the *Varia Carmina*, bears the title *Ad magnificum et nobilem virum dominum Adelbertum de Rotberg . . . pro virginalis conceptionis defensione, contraque maculistarum virginis Mariae furorem invectio.* Zarncke, pp. 175ff. See also Brant's German lines quoted by Schmidt, I, 269.

36. Schmidt, I, 218f.

37. *Ibid.*, I, 218–25.

38. The revocation is printed by Strobel, pp. 28ff.

39. Schmidt I, 228–30. The lines quoted are on p. 229, note 132: "Nec recte a Musis posthac Philomuse voceris,/ Sed eris, seu philomerda magis." The Latin poem is spiced with Greek words and lines. Brant sent Zasius these verses on September 26, 1505.

40. This honor is usually conferred upon Wimpheling's *Stylpho* (1480), which however hardly belongs in that class.

41. It may be preserved in German as the *Histori Herculi* by the Nuremberg Humanist Pangratz Bernhaubt, called Schwenter. See Dieter Wuttke in *Beihefte zum Archiv für Kulturgeschichte*, Heft 7, Cologne, 1964. On Brant's play see also Chapter 3 below.

42. Strobel, pp. 30ff.: "das dem Papst, dem König, dieser Statt oder sonst einer Statt, oder auch einzelnen Personen schädlich sei, ohne Erlaubniss des Meisters und Raths."

43. Strobel, p. 31: "Quare suppliciter rogo ut apud dominum inter-cedatis, ex mea parte, ut exemplar restituat et si vestrae dominationi placuerit exprimatur, vel alio in loco vendatur" ("Where I humbly request that you intercede with the master on my behalf that he return the copy and, if it please your authority, that it be printed or sold elsewhere").

44. However, Brant and Reuchlin always remained friends. In the letter of January 13, 1500, Brant wrote to him "you are dearer than life to me"; and on November 14, 1514, at the time of the dispute with the Cologne Dominicans, Reuchlin was concerned about Brant's silence and hoped that the reason was not the false accusation that Reuchlin had antagonized the Church. "Don't desert me, dear Titio!" he pleads. See Schmidt, I, 227.

45. The letter is dated September 21, 1514: "I love him, I revere him, it has been my good fortune to see him, embrace him." See Schmidt, I, 232. This letter is appended to Erasmus' *De duplici copia verborum et rerum* (Strasbourg, 1514). In Latin the pertinent passage reads: "Nam Sebastianum Brant, ut eximium, extra omnem et ordinem et aliam porro; quem ego virum, mi Wimphelinge, tanti facio, sic amo, sic suspicio, sic vereor, ut magna quaedam foelicitatis pars accessisse mihi videatur, quod illum coram intueri, coram alloqui et amplecti contigerit." See *Opus Epistolarum Des. Erasmi Roterdami, denuo recognitum et auctum par* P. S. Allen, II, Oxoni (Clarendon), 1910, p. 21.

46. Among Brant's correspondents were Wimpheling, Reuchlin, Bergmann, Amerbach, Tritheim, Zasius, Peutinger, Purckheimer, Hermannsgrün, Potken, and Rinck. His extant letters are scattered and have not yet been collected. The University of Basel has one letter (*Sig. Mscr.* GII, 32), published in vol. I of the Amerbach correspondence, ed. by Alfred Hartmann (1942) as No. 207. It also has a photograph of a letter to him by Zasius of 1505; the original was sold to a private collector in 1960. The Strasbourg National and University Library has copies of over one hundred Brant letters that were available to Charles Schmidt (No. 3878); the municipal archives of Strasbourg possess other Brant letters or copies, some on loan from the St. Thomas archives. The Municipal Library (Vadiana) in St. Gall has a paper manuscript of the fifteenth century containing copies of letters, excerpts, and poems of Brant; some of these were published by Geiger in his edition of the Reuchlin letters, the rest are still unpublished. See Chapter 1, note 16. Dieter Wuttke of Bonn is planning an edition of Brant letters.

47. See J. Janitsch, *Das Bildnis Seb. Brants von Albrecht Dürer.*

48. Strobel, p. 33, note 47: "Ab isto tempore usque Simphor. ab-

sens fui, missus Gandav. ad Caes. maiest. Redii sanus et incolumis, gratiam Caesaris adeptus ex congratulatione. Laus Deo optimo maximo!"

49. Strobel, pp. 34ff.: "so würdt solch werwer überall,/so gruselich Zufall uff erstan,/ alsz ob all welt solt undergan./ Gott helff der hayligen Christenheit!/ O Pfaffheit lasz dirs sin geseit,/ dasz du nit werdtst vertilckht, zerstreit./ Gott woll das nit ein Erdflus komb,/ die alles Erdtrich umb und umb/ versenckht, oder der Heiden schar/ in aller Christenheit umbfar,/ die understandt verderben gar/ disze vilfaltig . . . aber alsz man sich schickht uff erdt/ mit laster, sündt, schandtlicher geberdt,/ besorg dasz es böszer werdt./ Ohn zwiffel würdt gros enderung/ in höhe und nider, alt unnd jung,/ in frucht, visch, vöglen, thier und lüth. . . ." Reprinted by Zarncke, pp. 161f. See also the Latin poem "Epicedion" composed after Maximilian's death, discussed in Chapter 6 (Zarncke, p. 198). Here he fears the fall of the Empire, just as Von Andlau had in *Libellus de Caesarea monarchia* (1460) and Brant had in 1498 in the poem "De corrupto ordine . . ."

Chapter Three

1. Both epigrams are printed by Zarncke, p. 194.

2. Both versions can be found in Zarncke, p. 194.

3. Zarncke prints this thirty-line poem on pp. 190ff. The pertinent passages read: "Spe rex vivo quidem, sors licet invideat./ Cum regem fortuna potes fecisse poetam,/ Non tamen efficies, rex sit ut ille diu. . . . Omnia cum demes forsan tamen ille manebo,/ Pauperibus vates pauper ut ante fui."

4. Zarncke prints both versions, pp. 181ff. From the first: "Alter Caesareo sed semine missus ab alto,/ Maximiliane quidem pacifer orbis ades." From the second: "Nil modo Romano fas est obsistere regi,/ Unum eris imperii, Maximiliane, decus."

5. Zarncke, p. 186: "Nulla fides his sit, pereant! haec foedera sunto!/ Supplicio poenas quas meruere luant./ Phas et iura sinunt urbs haec patiatur aratrum/ Aequaturque solo terra nefanda suo . . ./ Germani antiqui sic sic iuvat esse decori,/ Imperio virtus pristina visque monet."

6. Schmidt in his bibliographical index (II, 350) leaves the question of date open.

7. The original Latin *Cato* is by a cleric, probably of very early date (eighth century?) and was translated into German for the first time in the thirteenth century. On *Facetus* and *Thesmophagia* see note 34 to Chapter 1. Brant's translation of *Moretus* seems to have been the first; at least, no previous translations are known. The dedication to Onuphrius was added for publication.

8. Lines 90–95 of the last strophe read: "Den gloub mit wercken stercken/ Und zieren, unsz zu füren/ zu selgem end behend,/ nach disem ellend/ uns werd geben das wir schweben/ by dir und leben." This is from the version used by Zarncke. ("To strengthen faith with works/ And adorn it, to lead us/ quickly to a blessed end. After this wretched exile/ May it be granted us to stay/ With thee and live there"). Musical notes for *Ave praeclara* are to be found in **Heitz's** *Flugblätter des Sebastian Brant*.

9. In Chapter 1, p. 39 the probable chronological sequence in which these works were translated was given, viz., *Cato, Facetus, Moretus,* and *Thesmophagia*. To the "internal evidence" adduced there can be added the usage of the word *narr*. In *Cato, tor (dor)* is used interchangeably with *narr* and in a general meaning not yet consonant with its use in the *Narrenschiff*. In *Facetus,* too there is no suggestion of the sense found in the *Narrenschiff*. It means simply a dull-witted person. Cf. lines 108 and 484 (Zarncke, pp. 138 and 141). But in *Moretus, narr* is not only used more frequently (and *tor* not at all), but also to contrast with *wysz* ("wise man"). Cf. 11. 342–53, Zarncke, p. 145. Moreover, if *Cato, Facetus,* and *Moretus* were actually produced in translation when they were published (*Cato* probably in 1496, the other two more definitely in that year), their great similarity would make a single publisher likely. But this is not the case. Furter published *Cato;* Bergmann, the other two.

10. I follow Schmidt as regards the date: "vers 1496" (II, 347). For no apparent reason Weller calls this a later edition, assigning it to 1502. Goedeke, *Grundriss,* I, 388, is under the impression, erroneous I think, that Bergmann's edition of 1498 is the oldest.

11. Zarncke p. 137: "Nach mym vermögen wirt gemert/ Was Catho nyt hat alls gelert."

12. In 1880 Hugo Lemcke published both the original and Brant's translation. See note 34 to Chapter 1.

13. Stockmeyer and Reber in their *Beiträge zur Basler Buchdruk-kergeschichte* (Basel, 1840), p. 49, take this woodcut to be a likeness of Brant himself.

14. In the *Narrenschiff,* Chapter 65, Brant seems to speak against astrology and the belief in portents, but in his edition of the *Revelations of Methodius* (an early Greek bishop and martyr), first published by Furter in 1498, he expresses the opposite view. Perhaps, however, in the *Narrenschiff* his opposition is directed more against fools who misuse portents and revelations for their own specific purposes. This is indicated by the opening lines: "Fool he who'd promise more than he/ Can keep with full propriety,/ More e'en than he'd desire to do./ Physicians well may promise you,/ But many fools will promise more/

Than all the world can hold in store." ("Der ist ein narr der me ver-
heiszt/ Dann er jn sym vermögen weisszt/ Oder dann er zu tun hat
mut/ Verheissen ist den ärtzten gut/ Aber eyn narr verheisszt eyn tag/
Me dann all welt geleysten mag." However, he goes on to scoff at
"worsagen . . . vogelgschrey . . . treümerbuch . . . der schwartzen
kunst" ("fortune telling . . . bird cries . . . dream book . . . nec-
romancy"), ll. 46ff. Eberth, in *Die Sprichwörter des Sebastian Brant,*
believes that Brant was never superstitious.

15. Berler's Chronicle is in the *Code historique et diplomatique de
la ville de Strasbourg,* II, 103. Merian is cited in Poggendorf's *Annalen
der Physik,* CXXII (1864), 182. The several woodcuts prepared for
this broadside, as well as for some fifteen others, are reproduced in
Paul Heitz's *Flugblätter des Sebastian Brant.*

16. Reprinted in Rochus von Liliencron, *Die historischen Volkslieder
der Deutschen* II, 310ff., No. 183. The woodcut is reproduced by
Heitz. See note 8 above and note 33 to Chapter 1.

17. Zarncke, p. 182: "Mitis Onofri,/ Sedulus ora,/ Qui tua psallo/
Facta decora:/ Fac loca vitans/ Inferiora/ Par tibi fiam/ Mortis in
hora."

18. This poem was reprinted in the periodical *Alsatia* in 1875, p. 61.
The woodcut that went with it, as well as the one to the poem on
Onufrius just discussed, has been reproduced by Heitz.

19. Published in *Der ewigen wiszheit Betbüchlein* (Basel, 1518)
and republished by Wackernagel, *Das deutsche Kirchenlied* II, 1099
(the first volume, p. 226, contains the Latin version).

20. Zarncke, p. 184: "O patria, o felix Germania si tibi reges/ Aut
fortuna pares aut deus ipse daret./ Credo equidem cunctus nostris sub
legibus orbis/ Iamdudum foret."

21. See Zeydel, "Sebastian Brant and the Discovery of America,"
in *The Journal of English and Germanic Philology,* XLIII, 410ff.

22. Fol. 134 v.: "qui sua eruditione atque lucubratione Basileam
inclytam Germaniae urbem mirum in modum exornat."

23. Fol. 133 v.: "Trium principalium linguarum Hebraicae scilicet
sit et Chaldaicae: Graecae pariter et latinae interpres peritissimus.
Gallicanae etiam atque politioris linguae nostrae vernaculae imprimis
clarus. Etiam in divinis scripturis secretariusque in saecularibus libris
eruditissimus. . . . multa praeterea utilitati nostrae communi e graeco
in latinum vertit opuscula: Xenophontis apologiam per Socrate. . . .
Monomachiam Iliados Homeri de Paridis et Menelai duello in lingua
Germanica metrice."

Chapter Four

1. One, entitled *Die acht Schalkheiten* ("Eight acts of Roguery"), is very early, dating from about 1450. Each of these broadsides or handbills shows a fool bearing a couplet in a scroll. Some have believed that Brant was the author of one such series. In two articles, Zarncke described an octet of sheets that he discovered many years after the publication of his *Narrenschiff* edition; the first appeared in Naumann's *Serapeum*, the second as a pamphlet *Zur Vorgeschichte des Narrenschiffs*. These articles are in the Zarncke collection of Cornell University.

2. In Chapter 57 of the *Narrenschiff* Brant refers to it, and in Chapter 108 he speaks of it and the *Schluraffen* ship. The term *Schluraffe* probably derives from *slur*, "lazy," and *affe*, "ape."

3. *Studies in the Literary Relations of England and Germany in the Sixteenth Century.*

4. The first edition presents a haphazard mixture of Roman and Gothic type, apparently because the Bergmann shop still lacked sufficient types of any one font.

5. Brant refers in it to the completed work. The second edition (1495) contains two new chapters.

6. Published by Attendorn in Strasbourg. See Zeydel's *The Ship of Fools,* pp. 11ff., and the notes there.

7. The details are given in Zeydel, *op. cit.,* p. 13f.; see the notes there for bibliography.

8. Editions of the "Totentanz" appeared about 1488 in Ulm (Johann Zainer?), about 1492 in Mainz (Jacob Meydenbach?), in 1487 in Lübeck (Matthaeus Brandis), and again in 1489 and 1496 in Lübeck (Mohnkopf). This information was kindly supplied by Charles E. Weber of Louisiana State University.

9. This technique reminds one of the *Arbor Amoris* tractates, very popular in Brant's day. One of his Basel professors, Johannes Ulrich Surgant, wrote a similar work for preachers, *Manuale Curatorum,* just before his death in 1503. These tractates are devotional religious texts originally constructed on the model of a tree—a type of ancient symbolism—presenting a theme (the root of the "tree") in the form of a biblical quotation, which in turn, through exegesis, is illustrated (here follow the trunk and branches) by other biblical passages, authorities, allegories, sayings, and examples. This process was known in Latin as *arborisare.* See the monograph of Urs Kamber, *Arbor Amoris, der Minnebaum* (Berlin, 1964). But Brant does not necessarily satisfy all the demands of "arborizing," although the rhetorical technique of *expolitio*

that he uses (see below) is related to it. Perhaps he wanted to combine the two.

10. *Die Amerbachkorrespondenz,* im Auftrag der Kommission für die öffentliche Bibliothek der Universität Basel bearbeitet und herausgegeben von Alfred Hartmann, 1. Band, Basel, 1942, No. 60, p. 67.

11. The following sections, dealing with the structure of the *Narrenschiff* in accordance with Roman rules of rhetoric, the coordination of chapters, and Roman satire are based chiefly on the researches of Ulrich Gaier, the results of which are to appear in an article, "Rhetorische Form in Seb. Brants Narrenschiff" in *Deutsche Vierteljahrschrift für Literaturwissenschaft und Geistesgeschichte* and in two books of studies on Brant to be published by Niemeyer in Tübingen.

12. *Neophilologus* XLIII (19, 207–21).

13. "Die Narrensatire als Weg der menschlichen Selbsterkenntnis bei Seb. Brant."

14. See Zarncke, pp. 121ff., ll. 9ff.: "Perspicimus cunctos sine lege atque ordine, remos/ Traxisse, et velis non posuisse modum/ Atque ideo in Scyllam, Syrtes, brevia, atque Charybdim/ Vortice detrusos naufragiumque pati." Ll. 13ff.: "stultos/ Invenio cunctos hoc periisse modo:/ Quod praetergressi legemque modumque, viamque/ Quam deus et rerum dictitat ordo decens./ Omnia quae in caelo, aut terris, vel in aequore vivunt/ Ordine servantur."

15. *Die Holzschnitte zu Sebastian Brants Narrenschiff.* Lemmer reproduces one hundred and twenty-one cuts with the floral borders.

16. As early as 1837, when the cuts were first mentioned in modern times, Karl Friedrich von Rumohr linked them with Dürer. In 1892 Daniel Burckhardt, in *Dürers Aufenthalt in Basel 1492–1494,* mentioned Dürer again as the master, but this was emphatically rejected by W. Weisbach in 1896 in *Studien zur deutschen Kunstgeschichte* and in *Die Basler Buchillustration.* There the matter rested for some time. Then, in 1943, Erwin Panofsky in *Albrecht Dürer* (Princeton, 1943), II, 53, attributed some of the cuts to Dürer. Finally in 1951 Friedrich Winkler in *Dürer und die Illustrationen zum Narrenschiff* proved that this master, the master of the Bergmann shop, as he has been called, was none other than Dürer. He showed that Dürer was not in Italy but in Basel from the spring of 1492 to the autumn of 1493, and that from there he went to Strasbourg. Helmut Rosenfeld, in vol. 5, *Verfasserlexikon des deutschen Mittelalters,* is not aware of recent research in this field.

17. See W. Fraenger, *Altdeutsches Bilderbuch: Hans Weiditz und Sebastian Brant.*

18. On this subject see also H. Lüdecke, *Albrecht Dürers Wanderjahre.*

19. See Strobel, pp. ix–xiii; Zarncke, pp. 267–91; H. D. Learned, *The Syntax of Brant's Narrenschiff;* W. K. Legner, *The Strong Verb in Sebastian Brant's Narrenschiff;* P. Claus, *Rhythmik und Metrik in Sebastian Brant's Narrenschiff;* and A. Heusler, *Deutsche Versgeschichte* III, paragraphs 911ff.

Chapter Five

1. The facsimile editions of Schultz and Koegler, both of 1913, use the Berlin copy as a basis. As noted in the text below, Lemmer's edition of 1962 uses chiefly the Dresden copy.

2. Not even Jacob Grimm had read the *Narrenschiff* before the appearance of Strobel's edition.

3. Zarncke, Goedeke (1872), and Bobertag (1889) copy at least one misprint of Strobel. See Zeydel, *The Ship of Fools*, p. 23, note 30. Zarncke also ignores Strobel's list of errata, and Bobertag ignores Zarncke's list!

4. Zeydel's modern English translation, frequently referred to, first appeared in 1944, was republished in 1962 (paperback), and again in 1966. See Bibliography.

5. By Lev Penkovsky (Gosudarstvennoe Izdatelstvo Chudozestvennoj literatury). This work, beautifully printed, has a brief introduction, reproduces only about one-half of the original text, is a verse translation, and contains the pertinent woodcuts but no bibliography.

6. In his second edition he added Chapter 75 in the fourfoot trochaic meter of the vagabond poets.

7. Both editions have been republished, the first by Herman Brandes, the second by Carl Schröder.

8. Copies are to be found in the British Museum and in the Saxon state library in Dresden.

9. Paris, 1822–1828, IV, 233.

10. Pompen refutes the old notion that Brant's original German directly influenced the foreign adaptations.

11. For a fuller discussion of Marchand, his version, and its history, see John R. Sinnema, *A Critical Study of the Dutch Translation of Sebastian Brant's "Narrenschiff,"* also Sinnema's "The German Source of the Middle Dutch 'Der zotten ende des narren scip.'"

12. The new catalogue of the British Museum records these.

13. As early as 1500, Badius published a Latin imitation of the *Narrenschiff*, partly in prose and partly in verse, but limited to the follies and foibles of women. It appeared in Paris in 1501. Wimpheling published a new edition in Strasbourg.

14. Barclay's chapter "Of Foles that are Overworldly," for example,

is based upon an entirely different source: a Latin poem of Robert Gaguinus, which Badius had used in his Latin rendering of 1505.

15. See Fedor Fraustadt, *Über das Verhältnis von Barclays "Ship of Fools" zur lateinischen, französischen und deutschen Quelle.* This work has not lost its value, but the book of Pompen is more up-to-date.

16. Edinburgh and London. Also in New York.

17. On the differences between Brant and Murner see M. Spanier's introduction to the *Narrenbeschwörung* (Halle, 1894).

18. Stuttgart; Scheible. Another "continuation," by a person calling himself F. Idus, appeared in Düsseldorf in 1886.

19. For nineteenth-century reprints of *Le droit chemin* see Zeydel, *The Ship of Fools*, p. 36, note 39.

20. On the popularity of Balsac's work and its influence on Copland see Zeydel, *op. cit.*, p. 37, note 41.

21. See his article "The Evolution of a Sixteenth-Century Satire."

22. It appeared in *Lateinische Literaturdenkmäler* herausgegeben von Max Herrmann, No. 10, edited by Karl Wotke, Berlin, 1894.

23. See A. W. Ward on Barclay in *The Dictionary of National Biography*, London, 1921, I, 1076ff.

24. See the article of W. G. Moore referred to in note 21 above, also the same writer's "Robert Copland and his Hye Way" in *Review of English Studies* VII (1931), 406ff.

25. Pompen, *op. cit.*, p. 298, is mistaken in saying that Erasmus did not know the *Narrenschiff.*

26. See Max Radlkofer, *Brants Narrenschiff, Murners Narrenbeschwörung, Erasmi Stultitiae laus, literarischhistorische Parallele;* and Hermann Schönfeld, "Die kirchliche Satire und religiöse Weltanschauung in Brants *Narrenschiff* und Erasmus' *Narrenlob*, resp. in den Colloquia"; see also Charles E. Weber, "Sebastian Brant's *Narrenschiff* as a Source for Erasmus's *Stultitiae laus*" (unpublished Master's thesis), Cincinnati, 1950. Radlkofer's and Schönfeld's contributions retain value only because of the materials they present.

27. This paragraph summarizes the argument of Gaier in a forthcoming book already referred to.

Chapter Six

1. *Verfasserlexikon des deutschen Mittelalters*, V (Nachträge), cols. 107ff. See also the end of Chapter 3 for a discussion of the various types of early works written by Brant.

2. Latin works of this type were mentioned at the beginning of Chapter 2. A still later German example deals with a frightening constellation (1504): *Von der wunderlichen zamefügung der öbersten Planeten* ("Of the strange conjunction of the upper planets").

3. The work as a whole has not been republished, but this poem was incorporated in the *Varia Carmina*, and part of it is in Zarncke, p. 185. The lines quoted read: "Perge igitur rex sancte cito, te fulmen acerbum/ Turcorum voluit maximus esse Deus,/ Qui stabile efficiat regnum tibi sceptra beando/ Sub pede dum teneas saecula cuncta. Vale.

4. Ll. 50ff.: Jetz sint die Türcken also starck/ Das sie nit hant das mer alleyn/ Sunder die Tunow ist jr gemeyn/ Und dunt eyn jnnbruch wann sie went. . . .

5. Ll. 91ff.: Die porten Europe offen syndt/ Zu allen sitten ist der vyndt/ Der nit schloffen noch ruwen dut/ In dürst allein, noch Christen blut. . . .

6. Ll. 121ff.: Eyn yeder fürst, der gansz bricht ab/ Das er dar von eyn fäder hab,/ Dar umb ist es nit wunder grosz/ Ob joch das rich sy blutt, und blosz. . . .

7. Ll. 211ff.: Es loszt sich eben sorglich an/ Leb ich, jch man noch manchen dran/ Und wer nit an myn wort gedenck/ Die narren kappen, ich jm schenck.

8. For a detailed discussion of the religious poetry in the *Varia Carmina* see *Sebastian Brant: Studies in Religious Aspects of His Life and Works with Special Reference to the Varia Carmina* by Sister Mary Alvarita Rajewski; also *Brant and Marian Poetry* by Sister A. M. Humbert. Brant also has warm praise of Mary in the edition of the *Hortulus rosarum* ("Garden of roses") of Thomas à Kempis, published by Bergmann in 1499. The passage quoted in the text is from poem 2 (Zarncke, p. 176): "Atque utinam videant mea saecula gentibus olim/ Promissum pariet quem pia Virgo Deum."

9. Zarncke, p. 188: "Gloria Petrarchae tanta est cumulata decore/ Ut sibi nil addi, nil minuive queat."

10. *Ibid.*: "Quicquid enim humanis potuit complectier usquam/ Usibus excultis arte vel ingenio,/ Hoc meus ingenue novit bonus ille poeta."

11. *Ibid.*: "Illic solus enim tot digna volumina scripsit,/ Quae vitiata quidem et sparsa fuere prius."

12. For further evidence of Brant's occupation with Petrarch see the Bibliography in Schmidt II, p. 359, No. 143, and pp. 372ff., Nos. 171ff.

13. The poem on Hrotsvit is in Zarncke, p. 189. Brant compares her fame with that of the imperial Ottos: "Contulit Otthonum vix tantum gloria laudis/ Saxonibus quantum femina sola suis." (Scarcely does the glory of the Ottos bring so much praise as this lone woman does to her Saxons.) On bibliographical information concerning editions of the *Varia Carmina*, see Schmidt II, 351f.

14. Zarncke, pp. 192ff. See also Fritz Husner, "*Sebastian Brant zum 500. Geburtstag*, Rede gehalten in der Aula der Universität am 22.

Herbstmond 1957 vor den Teilnehmern an der Jahresversammlung der Schweizerischen Bibliophilen Gesellschaft." Sonderdruck aus *"Stultifera navis,"* *Mitteilungsblatt der Schweiz. Bibl. Gesellschaft,* XIV (1957), 121.

15. Zarncke, p. 124, ll. 259ff.: "Haec sunt illa, deus quae fecit, lumina bina/ Magna quibus mundum lustret et irradiet."

16. See Chapter 4 above, p. 74.

17. Mentioned in *Varia Carmina,* No. 57, according to Zarncke's count (p. 187). See Schmidt II, 350f. The eight lines on Reuchlin's *Scenica progymnasmata,* not in the *Varia Carmina,* are in Zarncke, p. 195.

18. For fourteen of these see *Descensus Averno* by Anna Cox Brinton. These particular cuts illustrate the sixth book of the Aeneid. The frontispiece, which depicts Virgil as a recluse, was mentioned in Chapter 1.

19. This work seems little known as a product of Brant and can usually be found only under Hedio's name.

20. This copy is preserved among the St. Thomas papers now in the Strasbourg municipal archives.

21. Strobel, p. 306; Zarncke, p. 160: "Keyszer Julius was mild und recht;/ doch als er Rom acht für sin knecht/ unnd er allein wolt sin der Herr/ alsz ob kein Libertet mehr wehr/ wardt das schwehrlich an ihm gerochen,/ mit wunden viel zu todt gestochen."

22. Published in *Apparatus et instructus archivorum* (Strasbourg, 1713), pp. 15ff.

23. In *Beiträge zur deutschen Litteratur und Litterärgeschichte.*

24. Pp. xxxvi–xl and 154–58, partly transcribed from another seventeenth-century source. Schmidt II, 354f., recounts the somewhat involved story of how they were handed down.

25. *E.g.,* Zarncke, No. 22, p. xxxix: "Spiegel menschlichs Lebens," which Zarncke compares with Freidank 170, 14ff.

26. Compare Zarncke, No. 26, p. xxxix: "Ein zeichen der leichtfertigkeit/ Ist, Glauben eim Jeden Was er seyth" ("It is a sign of frivolity to believe everyone what he says"), and *Narrenschiff,* motto to Chapter 101: "Eyn zeichen der liechtferikeyt/ Ist, glouben was eyn yeder seit" ("He goes a careless, frivolous way/ Who credits what the others say").

27. "Wer Alle welt veracht mit Pracht/ Unndt uff sein Adel bocht mit macht/ Unndt sein herkommen nit betracht,/ Der würdt von aller Welt veracht,/ Dasz Er ein Narr sei tag und nacht:/ Gagag hat manche Gans gemacht" (Zarncke, p. 158).

28. On both the *Layen Spiegel* and the *Clagspiegel* see R. Stintzing, *Geschichte der populären Literatur des römischen-kanonischen Rechts*

in Deutschland, 1867, and *idem, Geschichte der deutschen Rechts-wissenschaft* I, 1880, 93ff.

29. Zarncke, p. 197: "Quicquid enim magni per tempora prisca seorsim/ Dii dederant aliis, cuncta ea solus habet." In the other poem referred to below (Zarncke, p. 197) Brant mentions in haphazard order Alexander, Pompey, Justinian, Constantine, the Aeacides (e.g., Achilles and Ajax), Charlemagne, Otto, Dagobert, Hector, Julius (Caesar), the Alcides (e.g., Hercules), the Scipios, and the Camilli, none of whom can compare with Maximilian.

30. Zarncke prints only four distichs of a poem addressed to Charles as king of Spain (1516). On the poem mentioned in the text see Schmidt II, 354, No. 125. It comprises twenty leaves.

Chapter Seven

1. *Medieval German Literature: A Survey* (Harvard University Press, 1962), p. 288.

2. *Studies in Philology* XLVIII, 30.

3. Quoted from Rudolf Stadelmann, *Vom Geist des ausgehenden Mittelalters: Studien zur Geschichte der Weltanschauung von Nicolaus Cusanus bis Sebastian Franck (Deutsche Vierteljahrschrift,* Buchreihe, 15. Band ([Halle, 1929]), p. 76. For other literature on the subject see Paul Mesterwerdt, *Die Anfänge des Erasmus: Humanismus und Devotio moderna* (Leipzig, 1917); and Gerhard Ritter, *Studien zur Spätscholastik* (three parts, 1921–1927: Sitzungsberichte der Heidelberger Akademie. Philosophisch-historische Klasse).

4. Strobel, *Das Narrenschiff,* pp. 5ff., and Zarncke, p. xxii: "*Ego equidem non modo non poetam me esse usquam praedicavi, sed ne poetriae quidem discipulum.*"

5. See note 14 to Chapter 3.

6. Strobel, *Beiträge zur deutschen Litteratur und Litterärgeschichte,* p. 37, and Zarncke, pp. 154ff.: "Nit lasz vom glauben dich abfüren,/ Ob man davon will disputieren;/ Sonder glaub schlecht einfeltiglich,/ Wie die heilig Kürch thut lehren dich./ Nimb dich der scharpffen Lehr nit an,/ Die dein Vernunfft nit mag verstahn./ Das Schäfflin schwembt offt usz an Stad,/ da der Helffant ertrinckht mitt schad,/ Niemandts nachfragen soll zu gnow/ dem glauben unnd seiner Ehefraw,/ dasz es zu letst ihn nit gerauw."

7. "Ich vörcht es kumen bald die tag/ Das man me nuwer mär werd jnn/ Dann uns gefall und sug zu synn. . . ."

Selected Bibliography

Concerning this Bibliography the reader is referred to the Preface. As a rule, the older literature on Brant, of the eighteenth and early nineteenth centuries, is not listed here but identified in the Notes and References whenever used.

1. General Literature on Brant

Strobel, A. W. "Einige Nachrichten über Sebastian Brants Lebensumstände und Schriften," In *Beiträge zur deutschen Litteratur und Litterärgeschichte* (Paris and Strasbourg), 1827.

Schmidt, C. "Notice sur Sébastien Brant," *Revue de l'Alsace,* III (1874).

Steinmayer, E. "Sebastian Brant," *Allgemeine deutsche Biographie,* III (1876), 256–59.

Schmidt, C. *Histoire littéraire de l'Alsace,* I (Paris, 1879), 189–333 (Bibliography, II, 340–73).

Schroeder, C. *Der deutsche Facetus* (Berlin, 1911) [Palaestra, Heft 86].

Heitz, P., ed. *Des Sebastian Brant Flugblätter,* ed., Franz Schultz (Strasbourg, 1915).

Fraenger, W. *Altdeutsches Bilderbuch: Hans Weiditz und Sebastian Brant* (Leipzig, 1930).

Brinton, A. C. *Descensus Averno,* Stanford University Press, 1930 [illustrations from Brant's Virgil: *Aeneid,* Book Six].

Westermann, R. "Sebastian Brant," *Verfasserlexikon des deutschen Mittelalters,* ed., Stammler, I (Berlin and Leipzig, 1933), cols. 276–89.

Gilbert, W. "The Culture of Basel in the Fifteenth Century: A Study in Christian Humanism." Diss. (Cornell), 1941.

Zeydel, E. H. "Johannes a Lapide and Sebastian Brant," *Modern Language Quarterly,* IV (1943), 209–12.

———. "Sebastian Brant and the Discovery of America," *Journal of English and Germanic Philology,* XLII (1943), 410–11.

Humbert, Sister A. M. "Brant and Marian Poetry," Diss. (Catholic University of America, Washington), 1944.

Rajewski, Sister M. A. "Sebastian Brant: Studies in Religious Aspects of his Life and Works, with Special Reference to the Varia Carmina." Diss. (Catholic University of America, Washington), 1944.

Gilbert, W. "Brant, Conservative Humanist," *Archiv für Reformationsgeschichte*, XLVI (1955), 145–67.

Rosenfeld, H. "Sebastian Brant" in *Verfasserlexikon des deutschen Mittelalters*, ed., Langosch, V, Nachträge, cols. 107ff.

2. Iconography of Brant

Janitsch, J. *Das Bildnis Sebastian Brants von Albrecht Dürer* (Strasbourg, 1906) [Studien zur deutschen Kunstgeschichte, Heft 74].

Springer, J., *Sebastian Brants Bildnisse* (Strasbourg, 1907) [Studien zur deutschen Kunstgeschichte, Heft 87].

3. On the *Narrenschiff*.

Editions since 1839

Das Narrenschiff. A. W. Strobel (Quedlinburg and Leipzig), 1839 [Bibliothek der gesamten deutschen National-literatur, 17].

Ibid. Friedrich Zarncke (Leipzig, 1854) [photomechanical reproduction: Hildesheim, 1961].

Ibid. Karl Goedeke (Leipzig, 1872) [Deutsche Dichter des 16. Jahrhunderts, 7].

Ibid. Franz Bobertag (Stuttgart, 1889) [Kürschners Deutsche Nationalliteratur, 16].

Ibid. Facsimile of the first edition of 1494 for the Gesellschaft der Bibliophilen, H. Kögler (Basel, 1913).

Ibid. Facsimile of the first edition of 1494 . . . with a postscript by Franz Schultz (Strasbourg, 1913).

Ibid. After the first edition (Basel, 1494) with the additions of the editions of 1495 and 1499, ed. Manfred Lemmer (Tübingen, 1962) [Neudrucke deutscher Literaturwerke, N. F. 5].

Translations into Modern German

Simrock, K. *Sebastian Brands Narrenschiff* (Berlin, 1872) [with the woodcuts].

Junghans, H. A. *Sebastian Brants Narrenschiff* (Leipzig, 1877), second edition, 1930 [Reclams Universalbibliothek].

Hirtler, F. *Sebastian Brant, Das Narrenschiff, die erbauliche satirische Weltbibel* (Munich, 1944).

Richter, M. *Sebastian Brant, Das Narrenschiff* (Berlin, 1958) [with 90 woodcuts].

Selected Bibliography

Modern English Translations

Zeydel, E. H. *The Ship of Fools by Sebastian Brant* (New York, 1944 [Columbia University Records of Civilization, 36]). A paperback edition (New York, Dover Publications, 1962). A hardback edition (New York, Octagon Press, 1966).

Modern Russian Translation

Penkovskij, Lev. Moscow, 1965 [contains the Prologue and fifty-four chapters with the woodcuts thereto].

The Low German Versions

Van Ghetelen. *Das Narrenschypp*, H. Brandes (Halle, 1914) [the Lübeck version of 1497].

————. *Das nye schip van Narragonien. Die jüngere niederdeutsche Bearbeitung von Sebastian Brants Narrenschiff*, ed. Schröder (Schwerin, 1892) [with the woodcuts; the Rostock version of 1519].

Literature Concerning the Narrenschiff

Zarncke, F. *Zur Vorgeschichte des Narrenschiffs:* 1. Mitteilung in *Serapeum* XXIX (1868), 49–54; 2. Mitteilung: Leipzig, 1871.

Schönfeld, H. "Die kirchliche Satire und religiöse Weltanschauung in Brants *Narrenschiff* und Erasmus' *Narrenlob*, resp. in den *Coloquia*," *Modern Language Notes* VII (1892), 39–46; 69–75; 173–74.

Genschmer, F. "The Treatment of the Social Classes in the Satires of Brant, Murner, and Fischart." Diss. (University of Illinois), 1934.

Bond, E. W. "Brant's *Das Narrenschiff*" in *Studia Otiosa: Some Attempts in Literary Criticism* (London, 1938), 18–42 [Reprinted from *Dublin Review*, 187, pp. 50–68].

Gumbel, H. "Brants *Narrenschiff* und Freidanks *Bescheidenheit:* Gestaltwandel der Zeitklage und der Wirklichkeit," *Beiträge zur Geistes- und Kulturgeschichte des Oberrheinlands*, Franz Schultz zum 60. Geburtstage gewidmet (Frankfurt/M., 1938), pp. 24–39.

Spamer, A. "Eine Narrenschiffspredigt aus der Zeit Sebastian Brants." *Otto Glauning zum 60. Geburtstag: Festgabe aus Wissenschaft und Bibliothek*, II (Leipzig, 1938), 113–30.

Zeydel, E. H. "Notes on Sebastian Brant's *Narrenschiff*," *Modern Language Notes*, LVIII (1943), 340–46.

————. "Some Literary Aspects of Sebastian Brant's *Narrenschiff*," *Studies in Philology*, XLII (1945), 21–30.

Böckmann, P. "Die Narrensatire als Weg der menschlichen Selbsterkenntnis bei Sebastian Brant," *Formgeschichte der deutschen Dichtung* I (Hamburg, 1949), 227–39.

Sobel, E. "Sebastian Brant, Ovid, and Classical Allusions in the *Narrenschiff*," *University of California Publications in Modern Philology*, XXXVI (1952), 429–40.

Gruenter, R. "Die 'Narrheit' in Sebastian Brants *Narrenschiff*," *Neophilologus*, XLIII (1959), 207–21.

Language and Style

Das Narrenschiff. Friedrich Zarncke (Leipzig, 1854), pp. 267ff.

Besson, P. *De Sebastiani Brant sermone* (Strasbourg, 1890).

Learned, H. D. *The Syntax of Brant's Narrenschiff* (Philadelphia, 1917).

Eberth, H. H. *Die Sprichwörter in Sebastian Brants "Narrenschiff."* (Bamberg, 1933).

Legner, W. K. "The Strong Verb in Sebastian Brant's Narrenschiff." Diss. (University of Pennsylvania), 1936.

Verse

Das Narrenschiff. Friedrich Zarncke (Leipzig, 1854), pp. 288ff.

Claus, P. *Rhythmik und Metrik in Sebastian Brants "Narrenschiff"* (Strasbourg, 1911) [Quellen und Forschungen, 112].

Heusler, A. *Deutsche Versgeschichte*, III (Berlin and Leipzig, 1929), paragraphs 911ff.

Woodcuts

Burckhardt, D. *Dürers Aufenthalt in Basel 1492–1494* (Munich, 1892).

Schreiber, W. L. *Manuel de l'amateur de la gravure*, II (Berlin, 1892).

Weisbach, W. *Der Meister der Bergmannschen Offizin und Albrecht Dürers Beziehungen zur Basler Buchillustration* (Strasbourg, 1896) [Studien zur deutschen Kunstgeschichte, Heft 6].

———. *Die Basler Buchillustration des XV. Jahrhunderts* (Strasbourg, 1896).

Friedländer, Max. *Repertorium für Kunstwissenschaft*, XIX (1896), 383ff.

Kautzsch, R. *Die Holzschnitte des Ritters vom Turn*, Basel, 1493 (Strasbourg, 1903) [Studien zur deutschen Kunstgeschichte, Heft 44].

Wölfflin, F. *Die Kunst Albrecht Dürers* (Munich, 1905).

Kögler, H. *Repertorium für Kunstwissenschaft*, XXX, 1907.

Wolters, M. *Beziehungen zwischen Holzschnitt und Text bei Sebastian Brant und Thomas Murner* (Baden-Baden, 1917).

[160]

Selected Bibliography

Winkler, F. *Dürer und die Illustrationen zum Narrenschiff* (Berlin, 1951).

Lüdeke, H. *Albrecht Dürers Wanderjahre* (Dresden, 1959).

Lemmer, M. *Die Holzschnitte zu Sebastian Brants "Narrenschiff"* (Leipzig, 1964).

Literary Influence of the Narrenschiff

Radlkofer, M. *Brants "Narrenschiff," Murners "Narrenbeschwörung," Erasmi "Stultitiae laus," literarisch-historische Parallele* (Programm Burghausen, 1877).

Herford, C. H. *Studies in the Literary Relations of England and Germany in the 16th Century* (Cambridge, 1886).

Fraustadt, F. *Über das Verhältnis von Barclays "Ship of Fools" zur lateinischen, französischen und deutschen Quelle*. Diss. (Strasbourg), 1894.

Rey, A. "Skelton's Satirical Poems in their Relation to Lydgate's *Order of Fools, Cock Lorell's Bote,* and Barclay's *Ship of Fools.*" Diss. (Bern), 1899.

Bjorkmann, E. *Bemerkungen zu der deutschen Bearbeitung des "Narrenschiffes"* (Uppsala, 1902).

Maus, T. "Brant, Geiler und Murner. Studien zum *Narrenschiff,* zur Navicula und zur Narrenbeschwörung." Diss. (Marburg), 1914.

Kärntner, J. "Des Jakob Locher Philomusus *Stultifera navis* und ihr Vernältnis zum *Narrenschiff* des Sebastian Brant." Diss. (Frankfurt), 1924.

O'Connor, D. "Notes on the Influence of Brant's *Narrenschiff* Outside Germany," *Modern Language Review,* XX (1925), 64–70.

Pompen, A. *The English Versions of the "Ship of Fools," a Contribution to the History of the Early French Renaissance in England* (London, 1925).

O'Connor, D. "Sebastien Brant en France au XVIᵉ siècle," *Revue de littérature comparée,* VIII (1928), 309–17.

Moore, W. G. "The Evolution of a Sixteenth-Century Satire." *A Miscellany of Studies in Romance Languages and Literatures presented to Leon E. Kastner,* M. Williams and A. de Rothschild (Cambridge, 1932), pp. 351–60.

Bauke, L. "Das mittelniederdeutsche *Narrenschiff* und seine hochdeutsche Vorlage," *Niederdeutsches Jahrbuch,* LVIII–LIX (1932–33), 115–64.

Sinnema, J. R. "A Critical Study of the Dutch Translation of Sebastian Brant's 'Narrenschiff.'" Diss. (University of Cincinnati), 1949.

———. "The German Source of the Middle Dutch 'Des zotten ende des narren scip,'" *On Romanticism and the Art of Translation:*

Studies in Honor of Edwin Hermann Zeydel, ed. G. F. Merkel (Princeton, 1956), 233–54.

Note: Barbara Könneker's *Wesen und Wandlung der Narrenidee im Zeitalter des Humanismus* (Steiner, Wiesbaden) appeared too late for consideration.

Index

Index